Coherent Materia Medica

Syllabus oriented, Key notes & Picture type

Hemant K. Sharma

Disclaimer

This book is based on keynotes symptoms of homoeopathic remedy and contain theoritical portion also. Useful for Homoeopathic students Particularly BHMS-I &BHMS-II year examination and understanding. And also useful for beginners in homoeopathic field.

Published by Notion press
Available from Amazon.com and other retail outlets

First Printing Edition, 2021
ISBN

Dedication

This book is dedicated to all the readers. Many of you were young teenagers with bright, beautiful eyes full of dreams for the future. I hope that in the years that have passed, you've all found your dreams and that the reality of them was even better than you'd hoped.

CONTENTS

Acknowledgments

History of all great works into witness that no great work was ever done without either active or passive support of a person 'surrounding and one's close quarters' thus is it not hard to conclude how active assistance from seniors and respected teachers could positively impact the execution of a coherent book on Materia Medica.

Last but not the least, I would also want to extend my appreciation to my dear dadaji and my parents and those who could not be mentioned here but have well played their role to love and inspire me behind the certain my closest soul person.

PART 1

Theoretical Part

CHAPTER ONE

GENERAL INTRODUCTION AND DEFINITION OF HOMOEOPATHIC MATERIA MEDICA

"A system of treatment based on similarity between symptoms of patient and those obtained during proving on healthy human beings".

The fundamental law of homoeopathy = "similia similibus curantur"(let likes be cured by likes).

Based on→ Therapeutic law of nature (§26) "A weaker dynamic affection is permanently extinguished in the living organism by a stronger one if the later (while differing in kind) is very similar to the former in its manifestations.

Father of homoeopathy→ Dr. Christian Fredrick Samuel Hahnemann (1755-1843).

Father of American homoeopathy→ Dr. Constantine Hering

Father of Indian homoeopathy→ Rajendra Lal Dutta

<u>Material Medica</u> –"It is a branch of medical science which deals with the origin of drugs, preparation of drugs, effect of drugs on human beings, their dosage and their mode of administration".

<u>Hom.Materia Medica</u> – According to Samuel **Hahnemann** in his Organon of Medicine **Aph.143,** homoeopathic materia medica is "a collection of real, pure, reliable modes of action of simple medicinal substances, a volume of book of nature."

"Store house of every action and reaction of drugs ".

Chapter Two

SOURCES OF HOMOEOPATHIC MATERIA MEDICA

Sources of Hom. Materia Medica–

1.) **Empirical source**→ Based on guesswork that attempts to explain general therapeutic properties of drugs.
Ex. i.) Dioscorides times (60A.D.) medicinal properties of drugs→ Diuretics, cathartic, antispasmodic etc. (No positive proof of that properties)
ii.) All red plants act better on blood.
iii.) If flowering period in summer then symptoms produced by drug prepared from same plant will have aggravation period in summer.

2.) **Knowledge of chemistry**→ It gives only clue about pharmacological action of drugs.
Because living beings and chemical factory both are different things.
So more the knowledge of chemical properties of a substance is not at all sure guide to it's application for curative purpose of sick individual.

3.) **Knowledge of toxicology**→ It is obtained from unnatural use and accident overdosing of drugs and their certain toxic effects.

4.) **Plant experimentations**→ It is gathered by studying the effects of drugs –on plant cell, plant chromosomes and plant chemistry. (on plant viruses & fungi also)

5.) **Animal experimentations**→ Only objective symptoms with pathological changes can be observed.

6.) **Healthy human drug proving**→By this method real and pure effects of drug substances can be obtained.
Most scientific and authentic way.
Real backbone of constricting Hom.Materia Medica.

7.) Clinical experience→ For reprove the drug substances at clinical level and add new clinical symptoms in materia medica that appears during the course of homoeopathic treatment applied for curative purpose.

CHAPTER THREE

SOURCES BOOKS OF HOMOEOPATHIC MATERIA MEDICA

<u>Sources books of Hom. Materia Medica</u> –

1.) FRAGMENTA DI VIRUBUS MEDICAMENTORUM POSITIVIS SIVE IN SANO CORPORE HUMANO OBSERVATATIS
Explation→Fragments on positive power of a drug i.e. to say their effect observed on healthy human being.
"Precursor of Materia Medica and Repertory".

2.) REINEARZNARZNEIMITTELLEHRE (By Dr.C.F.S Hahnemann)
Latin version→ Materia Medica Pura.

3.) DIE CHRONISCHEN KRANKHEITEN

4.) Encyclopedia of pure Materia Medica (T.F. Allen)

5.) Guiding symptoms of our Materia Medica (Dr. Constantine Hering)

6.) Manual of pharmacodynamics (By Richard Hughes)

7.) Cyclopedia of drug pathogenesis (By Richard Hughes and J.P. Duke)

8.) Dictionary of practical Materia Medica (J.H. Clark)

CHAPTER FOUR

DIFFERENT CLASSIFICATION OF MATERIA MEDICA

Different classification of Hom. Materia Medica –

Different types of Materia Medica have been developed in homoeopathy after Dr. Hughes criticised Hahnemann's anatomical classification of symptoms.

Dr. Hughes said that "It is as unnatural and artificial arrangement of the features of many allied morbid portraits as though an artist should paint a family group arranging all the eyes of all the members of the family, in one part of the picture, all the noses in another, the ears all together and so on".

1.) **Schematic (anatomical) Materia Medica→** Here drugs is studied organwise, like mind, head, nose, ear, abdomen and extremities.
   Ex. i.) Materia Medica Pura by Hahnemann.
   ii.) The Guiding symptoms of our Materia Medica by Hering.
2.) **Picture type Materia Medica→**Here drugs pathogenesis is presented (in abstract form) in a picture method to make Materia Medica more lively and easy to memories.
   Ex. i.) Homoeopathic Drug Pictures by M.L. Tyler.
   ii.) Homoeopathic Materia Medica of Graphical Drug Picture by Pulford.

3.) Comparative Materia Medica→ Here one drug is compared with the symptoms of another drug showing both similar and dissimilar symptoms, where dissimilar guides for differentiation to one from another.
Ex. i.) The comparative Materia Medica by Farrington.
ii.) Comparative Materia Medica by Gross.
Comparison level→
   a. At symptomatic level.
   b. At disease level.
   c. At organ level.
   d. At drug level.

4.) Therapeutic type of Materia Medica→ Here the drug symptoms are studied under the heading of different diseases. (Against holistic approach)
Ex. i.) HomoeopathicTherapeutics by Lilienthal.
ii.) Practical Homoeopathic Therapeutics by Dewey.

5.) Key-note Materia Medica→ Here the characteristic symptoms of each drug are presented. (Short, synthetic, comprehensive Materia Medica)
Ex. i.) Key-notes of Leading Remedies by H.C. Allen.
ii.) A Primer of Materia Medica by T.F. Allen.

6.) Physiological Materia Medica→ Here the drugs is studied in the manner as how it acts in the human system.
Ex. i.) Physiological Materia Medica by Burt.
ii.) A Manual of Pharmacodynamics by Hughes.

7.) Materia Medica of proving→ Materia Medica of proving contains drugs with their proving records on healthy human beings.
Ex. i.) Materia Medica Pura by Hahnemann.
ii.) Condensed Materia Medica by Hering.

8.) Clinical Materia Medica→Clinical Materia Medica is one of ways of studying Materia Medica. This is one subject which not just to be read but practiced.
Ex. i.) A Clinical Materia Medica by Farrington.
ii.) A Dictionary of Practical Materia Medica by Clarke.

9.) Combined Materia Medica→ Here drug is presented from various angles at a time, such as:

a) Physiological actions
b) Key-note symptoms
c) Symptoms from anatomical presentation
d) Symptoms picture type
e) Symptoms and drugs comparison
f) Therapeutic aspects.

10.) **Others**→ Psychoanalysis type, poetry type and pharmacodynamic type Materia Medica etc.

CHAPTER FIVE

SCOPE AND LIMITATION OF HOMOEOPATHIC MATERIA MEDICA

<u>**Scope and limitations of Hom. Materia Medica –**</u>

Scope of Hom. Materia Medica→

1.) Symptoms are collected by proving the drugs on healthy human beings of different ages, both sexes and different constitutions.

2.) We get a wide range of symptoms from one person to another during proving. (Greater scope in Hom. Materia Medica)

3.) There are several deep acting remedies in Hom. Materia Medica with wide sphere of action, so there is no difficulty in choosing the similimum.

4.) In drug proving, the medicine is withdrawn before any pathological changes take place.

5.) As drugs have been proved on human beings, the exact sensation, location, modalities and concomitants are collected. (Easy to find the exact similimum)

<u>Limitations of Hom. Materia Medica–</u>

1.) No proving records are available on pathological changes.
2.) Unimaginably vast.
3.) Irreversible pathology.
4.) In cases of acute immergencies→ The conditions where there is danger of life and death is nearby.
   Ex. In cardiac arrest, shock, syncope etc.
5.) Drugs which are partially proved.
6.) 30 modifications of the sensation of pain.
7.) Many of our provers are non medical men.
8.) Lack of sufficient female provers.
9.) No dependable pre operative, post operative or preventive drugs in our Hom. Materia Medica.
10.)   No dependable specifics.
11.)   There is no book on Materia Medica which we can claim to be complete and containing everything.

CHAPTER SIX

SOURCES OF DRUGS IN HOMOEOPATHY

<u>Sources of drugs in homoeopathy –</u>

1.) Plant kingdom
2.) Animal kingdom
3.) Minerals
4.) Nosodes
5.) Sarcodes
6.) Imponderabilia

CHAPTER SEVEN

BIOCHEMIC TISSUE SALTS

Biochemic Tissue Salts/Schuessler's salts/12- Tissue Remedy–

"The biochemic tissue salts also known as biochemic cell salts or Schuessler tissue salts".

The biochemic system of medicine is a simple and rational science of theraputics gifted to us by Dr. Wilhelm Schuessler from Germany.

The biochemic system of medicine derives it's name from the Greek word. ("Bios"→ meaning life and "Chemistry"→ meaning, a branch of natural science dealing with the composition of substances and their properties and reaction)

Biochemistry→ Chemistry of life.

It is the unique branch of theraputics. That is based on law of deficiency.

Prof. Moleschott, of Rome says, "The structure and vitality of the organs depend upon the presence of the necessary quantities of inorganic constituents".

The principle of this valuable science is based on the concept that deficiency of inorganic salts causes disharmony in the functioning of a cell, which when supplemented in the requisite proportion, restore this disharmonious functioning.

Thus the biochemic system of medicine assist the body's Natural efforts towards cure by supplementing these salts that are deficient in certain tissues.

Principles of the Biochemic cell salts→

1.) The body is made up of cells.

2.) Different kinds of cells build up the different tissues and organs of the body.

3.) The difference in cells are largely determined by the kind of inorganic salts which enter into there composition.

Biochemical remedy are→

1.) Inorganic cell salts (12 in number) → prepared by trituration.

2.) Rendered fine enough to be absorbed by delicate cells whenever needed.

3.) Binds with albumin to create form.

Name of 12-tissue salts→

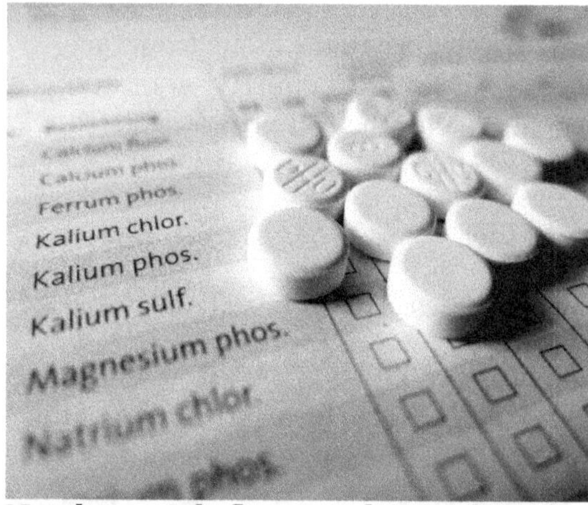

Number 1: Calc fluor – Calcium Fluoride – Tissue elasticity restorer

Number 2: Calc phos – Calcium Phosphate – Cell restorer

Number 3: Calc sulf – Calcium Sulphate – Blood purifier, purulent agent

Number 4: Ferr phos – Phosphate of Iron – Anti-inflammatory

Number 5: Kali mur – Potassium Chloride – Detoxifying agent

Number 6: Kali phos – Potassium Phosphate – Nerve and brain cell agent

Number 7: Kali sulf – Potassium Sulphate – Metabolism, pancreas conditioner

Number 8: Mag phos – Magnesium Phosphate – Pain and cramp killer

Number 9: Nat mur - Sodium Chloride – Water distributor

Number 10: Nat phos – Sodium Phospahte – Acidity neutraliser

Number 11: Nat sulf – Sodium Sulphate – Liver cleanser

Number 12: Silicea – Silicic Oxide – Skin and connective tissue conditioner

CHAPTER EIGHT
TRIOS OF REMEDY

Trios of remedy –

Trio of Thirstlessness: Apis, Aethusa, Pulsatilla.

Trio of Masturbation and Excessive venery: Nux vomica , Staphysagria , Bufo rana.

Trio of Croup: Aconite, Spongia, Hepar sul.

Trio of Restlessness: Arsenic, Aconite, Rhus tox.

Trio of Pain: Aconite, Coffea, Chamomilla.

Trio of Flatulence: Carbo veg, China, Lycopodium.

Trio of Burns: Sulfur, Arsenicum album, Phosphorous.

Trio of Condylomata: Thuja, Staphysagria, Nitric acid.

Trio of Offensiveness: Kreosote, Merc sol, Baptisia.

Trio of Cholera: Veratrum alb, Arsenic alb, Camphor.

Trio of Sleepiness: Ant tart, Gelsimium, Nux mos.

Trio of Offensive Urine: Benzoic acid, Nitric acid, Sepia.

Trio of Homoeopathic Last Aid: Carbo veg, Arsenic alb, Muriatic acid.

Trio of Paralysis: Causticum, Rhus tox, Sepia.

Trio of Ptosis: Causticum, Gelsimium, Sepia.

Trio of Prostration: Carbo veg, Arsenic alb, Muriatic acid.

Trio of Hyper- aesthesia: Plumbum, China,Capsicum.

Trio of Chronic Rheumatism: Causticum, Rhus tox, Sulphur.

Trio of Warts: Causticum, Thuja, Dulcamara.

Trio of Delirium: Belladonna, Hyoscyamus, Stramonium.

Trio of Convulsions: Cuprum met, Cicuta virosa, Causticum.

Trio of Liver Remedies: Chelidonim, Aur Mur, Leptandra Virginica.

Trio of Anti-Scrofulous Remedies: Baryta Carb, Iodium, Bromium.

Trio of Diarrhoea: Gambogia, Gratiola, Oleander.

PART 2

Homoeopathic Drug Picture

ACONITUM NAPELLUS

Common name–Monkshood

Family – Rannunculaceae

Constitution – Acute/ recent cases

Girls of full plethoric habit

Who lead→ a sedentary life

Appearance→ Dark hair & eyes + Rigid muscular fibre.

Mental general–

Great fear & anxiety of mind (**imp**)

Expressive of→ fear (**imp**)

Life is rendered miserable by→ fear (**imp**)

Fear of death→ during pregnancy (**imp**)

Afraid of → crowd & crossing street.

Predicts the day of death.

Restless, anxious, hasty, change position often.

Mental anxiety, worry, fear.

Music is→ unbearable→ makes sad.

Physical general –

Causation→ (**imp**)

Exposure to→ dry cold air, dry North or west wind.

Exposure to→ drafts of cold air.

Perspiration

Bad effect of→ checked perspiration.

For congestive stage of inflammation.

Pains→

Intolerable, insupportable.

Drive him→ crazy.

Very restless→ at night.

General modalities–

 Agg. → . Evening & night.

. In warm room.

. Rising from→ bed.

. Lying on→ affected side.

Amel. → . In open air.

Particulars –

Nervous system –

On rising from recumbent position→<u>faint</u>→ falls.

Fear to rise again.

Associated symptoms→ Vanishing of→ sight.

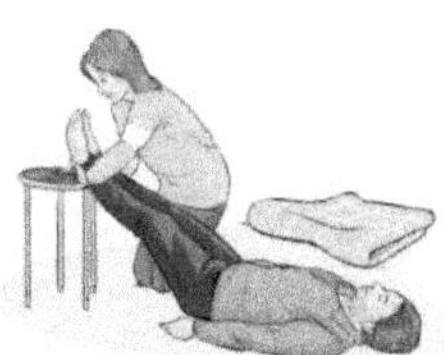

Unconsciousness.

Respiratory system –

Cough→. Croup

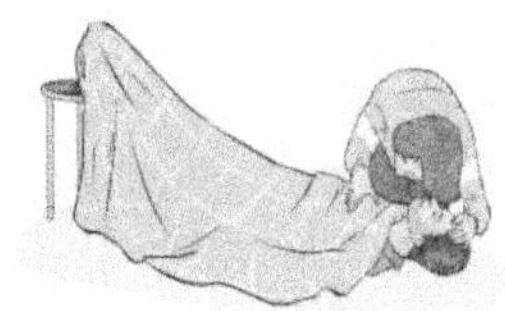

Dry, hoarse, suffocating.

Whistling sound→ on expiration.

Complaints → from causation.

Fever – (imp)

Never to control fever.

Injurious in first stage of typhoid fever.

In fever→ if prescribed→ bring eruption.

Face→ Red & pale ulternately.

Skin→ Dry & hot

Thirst→ Burning thirst.

Large quantities & cold water.

Female rep. System –

Amenorrhea (in young girl)→ after fright.

To prevent→ suppression of menses.

Aethusa Cynapium

Common name – Fool's parsley.

Family – Umbelliferae.

Constitution –

Especially→ for children

During→ dentition.

Children→ who can't bear milk.

In hot summer weather.

Mental general –

Idiocy.

Incapacity to think.

Confused.

Physical general –

Great weakness & drowsiness.

Unable to hold→ head.

Agg. → . After eating/drinking.

. After vomiting.

. After stool.

. After spasm.

Thirst→ completely absent.

General modalities –

Agg. → . After eating/drinking.

. After vomiting.

. After stool.

. After spasm.

Particulars –

Nervous system –

Epileptic spasm with→ . Clenched thumbs

Red face + Eyes turns downward**(imp)**

Foams→ at mouth.   Pupil→ Fix, dilated.

Jaws→ locked.   Pulse→ small, hard, quick.

Face –

Expression of→

Great anxiety + pain.

Drawn condition.

Well marked linea nasalis. **(Imp)**

Features→

Pain & anxiety.

Herpetic eruption→ on end of nose.

G.I.System –

Indigestion→ . In teething children.

Violent sudden vomiting→

Froath + Milky white substance + Yellow fluid.

Followed by→ . Curdled milk, cheesy matter.

Regurgitation of food 1 hr. Or so after eating.

Vomiting→. Copious, greenish.

Intolerance of milk→ can't bear milk in any form.

ALLIUM CEPA

Common name – Onion.

Family– Liliaceae.

Constitution –Phlegmatic patient.

Physical general –

Acute catarrhal inflammation of mucous membrane.

↑sed secration.

Bad effect of→ getting wet. (Causation)

General modalities – Agg. → . in evening, in warm room.

Amel. → . in cold room, open air.

Particulars –

Eyes – (imp)

Excessive lachrymation (watery).

Sensation→ . Burning. Bitting & smarting as from smoke.

Must rub the eyes.

Head–

Catarrhal dull headache + coryza.

Agg. → . In evening, in warm room.

Amel. → . In cold room, open air.

Headache ceases→ during menses.

Headache returns→ when flow disappears

Extremities –

Sore & raw spots→ on feet. . Especially→ heel.

. Cause→ friction.

Efficacious when feet are rubbed sore.

(Dioscorides)

Panaritia→ . Red streaks up the arm.

. Pain→ drive to despair.

G.I.System –

After→ forceps delivery.

Colic→ From: getting feet wet, overeating, cucumbers, salads.

Hemorrhoid.

Particular modality→ . **Agg.** →sitting.

. **Amel.** → moving about.

Nose –

Spring coryza.

Causation→ Damp, nort-easterly winds.

Lacrimation

Profuse & bland lachrymation.

Discharge→ . Burn & corrodes nose and upper lip.. Acrid watery.

. From→ tip of nose.

Nasal polypus.

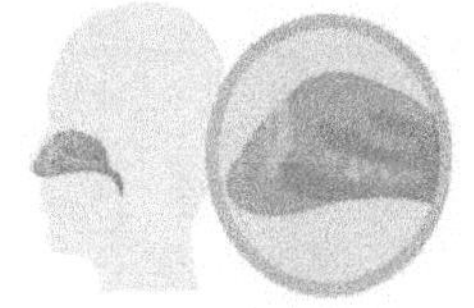

Female Rep. System – Phlebitis.

Perperal, After→ forceps delivery.

Resp. System –

Hay fever→ In August (every ear).

Violent sneezing.

. Causation→ 1. On rising from bed.

2. From handling peaches.

Catarrhal laryngitis.

. Cough→ grasp larynx. (seems cough would tear the larynx)

Nervous system –

Neuralgic pain. (Sensation→ Burning, stinging, like a long thread).

Site→ In face, head, neck, chest.

Traumatic chronic neuritis.

Neuralgia of stump after amputation.

ALOE SOCOTRINA

Common name→ Socotrina aloes

Family→ Liliaceae

Constitution→ Adapted to:

Indolent, weary persons, averse to mental or physical labor.

Mental labor fatigue.

Old people.

Women→ Relaxed & phlegmatic habit.

Mental generals→ Dissatisfied.

Angry about himself.

Angry about complaints. (Especially→ constipated)

General Modalities→ **Agg.**→ Early morning.

Sedentary life.

Hot dry weather.

After→ standing, walking, eating or drinking

Amel.→ Cold water.

Cold weather.

Discharge of→ flatus & stool.

Particulars→

Physical generals→

Diseases of mucous membrane.

Production of mucous in jelly like lumps.

Site→ Throat, Rectum.

Extreme→ Prostration + perspiration.

Affects→ mucous membrane of rectum.

Head→ Headache.

Site→ Across the forehead.

Sensation→ Heaviness of eyes and nausea.

Particular modality→

< every foot step.

< from heat.

Relief→ from cold application.

Alternating with lumbago after insufficient stool. **(imp.)**

Skin→ Itch appears each year. (As winter approaches)

Like Sulphur→ Many chronic diseases→ Developed suppressed eruption.

G.I.System→

Diarrhoea→ (imp.)

(Flatus+ stool passing sensation)

Hungry during diarrhoea.

Immediately after eating and drinking.

Want of confidence in sphincter ani.

Driving out of bed early in the morning.

Stool→ (imp.)

Before stool→ Rumbling, violent, sudden urging.

During stool→ Tenesmus, much flatus.

After stool→ Faintness.

Colic→ Type of pain→ cutting, gripping.

Site→ Lower portion of abdomen.

Excruciating→ Before & during stool.

Ceases→ After stool.

Profuse sweating and extreme weakness.

Obstinate constipation.

Flatus→ Offensive, burning.

Copious, much flatus + small stool.

Burning in anus.

Hemorrhoids→

Blue (like a bunch of grapes).

Constant bearing down→ in rectum.

Intense itching (Preventing sleep).

General modalities.

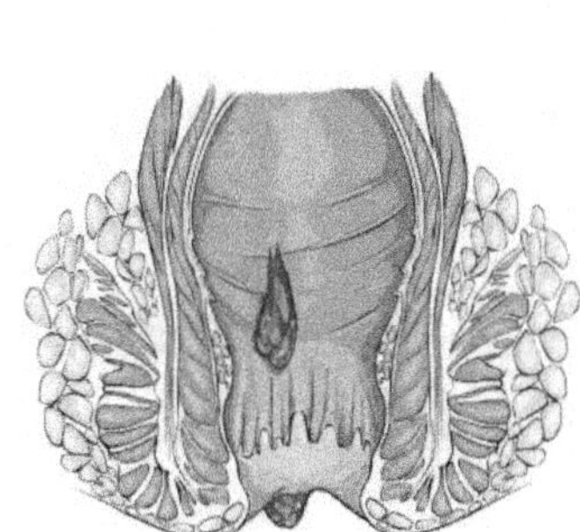

ANTIMONIUM CRUDUM

Common name→ Sulphide of Antimony.

Chemical formula→ SbS_3

Constitution→ Children.

Young people→ inclined to grow fat.

Extreme of life.

Old people→ Morning diarrhoea

Constipation

Alternate→ Diarrhoea & Constipation.

Pulse→ Hard + rapid.

Mental generals→ Child:

Freatful & Peevish

Can't bear to be touched or looked at

Sulky

Doesn't wish to speak

Angry→ At every little attention

Great→ sadness + weeping

Loathing life

Anxious, abject despair

Lachrymose mood

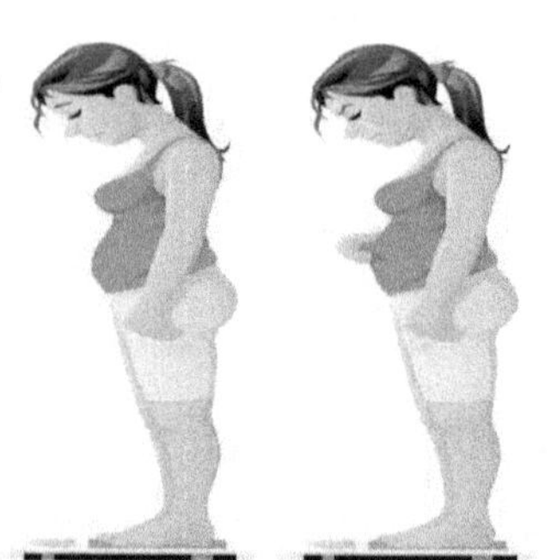

Sentimental mood→ in moon light (especially→ ecstatic love)

Bad effects of disappointed affection

Irresistible desire to talk in rhymes.

Physical general→ Sensitive→ to cold.

Desire (Longing) → Acids & pickles.

Can't bear heat of sun.

Ailments→ Sunburn

< over-heating near fire.

< over-exertion in the sun.

< in warm weather (exhausted)

Symptoms reappear→ (change locality, one side to another)

Aversion→ cold bathing.

Cold bathing causes→ violent headache& suppressed menses.

Colds from swimming / falling into water.

General modalities (imp.)→ **Agg.**→ After eating , cold baths, acid or sour wine.

After heat of sun or fire.

Extremes of cold or heat.

Amel.→ Open air.

During rest.

After a warm bath.

Particulars→ **Head**→ Headache

Causation→ River bathing, taking cold.

Alcoholic drinks, deranged digestion.

Acids, fat, fruits.

Suppressed eruption.

Throat→ Mucus→ in large quantity.

From posterior nares.

By hawking.

Skin (imp.)→ Abnormal growth.

Fingernails don't grow→ rapidly.

Crushed nails grow→ in split like warts + horny spots.

Respiratory system→ Loss of voice from→ overheated.

Whooping cough→ General modalities.

G.I.System→ Constant discharge of flatus.

Gastric complaints→ from overeating, stomach weak, digestion disturbed.

Sore in mouth

Mucous piles (ichorus, oozing, staining yellow)

Gastric & Intestinal affections→ from:

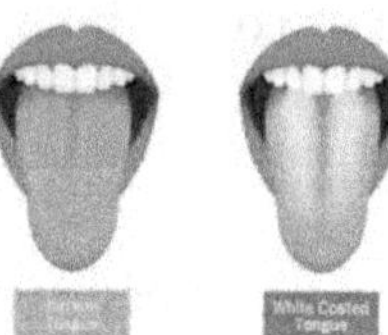

Bread, pastry, acids (esp.→ vinegar), sour or bad wine.

Red strand of remedy→ A thick milky white coating on the tongue. (imp.)

Belching testing ingesta.

ANTIMONIUM TARTARICUM

Common name→ Tartar emetic.

Constitution→ Persons→ Hydrogenoid Constitution of Grauvogl.

Mental generals→ Child:

Clings those around.

Wants to be carried.

Cries if anyone touches it.

Will not you feel the pulse.

Physical generals→ Great sleepiness.

Irresistible inclination to sleep.

Diseases originating→ Exposure in damp basement & cellars.

General modalities→ **Agg.**→ In damp & cold weather.

Lying down at night. Warmth room.

Change of weather→ in spring.

Amel.→ Cold open air.

Sitting upright. Expectorating.

Lying on→ Rt. Side.

Particulars→ **Mouth**→ Tongue→ coated, pasty, thick, white.

Reddend papillae + red edges + very red (dry in the middle)

Extraordinary craving→ forApples.

Face→ Cold. Blue, pale.

Covered with cold sweat.

G.I.System→

Vomiting→ any position

Except: lying on right side

Until he faints.

Associated symptoms→ Drowsiness & prostration.

Cholera morbus + diarrhea + cold sweat.

Respiratory system→ **(imp.)**

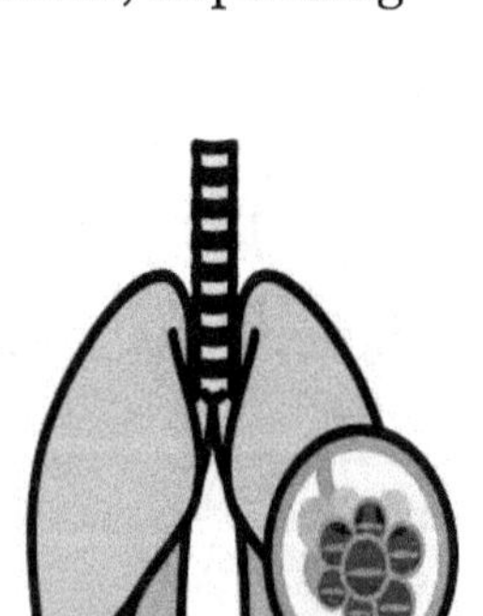

Depresses (through pneumogastric nerve) → Respiration, circulation.

When the patient coughs large correction of mucous in the bronchi.

Asphyxia→ Mechanical, drowning, mucous in bronchi, impending paralysis of lungs.

Foreign body→ (in larynx/ trachea)

Associated symptoms→ Drowsiness, coma.

Asphyxia neonatrum. (Relieves the death rattle)

Icterus + pneumonia (Especially→ Rt. Lung)

In spring & autumn. (Cough→ Worse)

APIS MELLIFICA

Common name→ Poison of the honey bee.

From→ Apium virus (whole poison of honey bee animal)

Constitution→ Strumous constitution.

Glands→ Enlarged, indurated, scirrhus/ open cancer.

Women→ Widows.

Children & girls.

Generally careful.

Awkward.

Let things fall while handling them.

Mental generals→

Ailments→ Jealousy, fright,

rage, vexation, bad news.

Irritable nervous→ hard to please.

Weeping disposition.

Can't help crying.

Discouraged.

Despondent.

Sudden.

Shrill.

Piercing screams from children→ During: walking or sleeping.

Physical generals→

Extreme senstiveness→ to touch.

Pain→ Sensation→ Burning, stinging, sore,

Suddenly migrating. (From one part→ another)

Particular modalities→ Pain aggravated by:

<coughing

<walking& changing position

<sitting erect.

General modalities→ **Agg.**→ After sleeping.

Closed. (Warm or heated room)

Amel.→ Open air, cold water/ bathing.

Uncovering, moistening.

Particulars→

Eyes→ Edema.

Bag-like puffy swelling. (Site→ under the eyes)

Skin→Bad effect of→ Acute exanthema.

Suppressed (imperfectly developed)→ measles, scarlatina, urticaria.

Fever→ Intermittent fever.

Chill 3p.m. + thirst.

<warm room.

<from ext. heat.

Extremities→ Edema

Site→ Hands + feet.

Dropsy without thirst. (imp.)

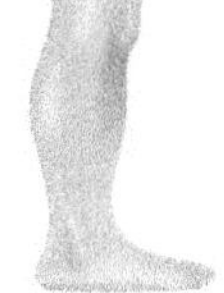

Urinary system→ Incontinence of urine.

Irritation of parts.

Retain urine at a moment.

Urine passed→ scalds severely, painful,

Scanty, bloody.

G.I.System→

Constipation→ Sensation→ as if something tight would break.

Causes→ if much efforts used.

Diarrhoea→ Drunkards.

In eruptive disease.

Suppressed eruption.

Involuntary. (As though anus was wide open)

ARGENTUM NITRICUM

Common name→ Silver nitrate.

Chemical formula→ AgO, NO_5

Constitution→ Always think of Arg. nitricum.

On seeing withered.

Dried up.

Old-looking patients.

Mental generals→ Apprehension→ Diarrhoea sets in. (When ready for church/ opera)

Time passes slowly.

Impulse.

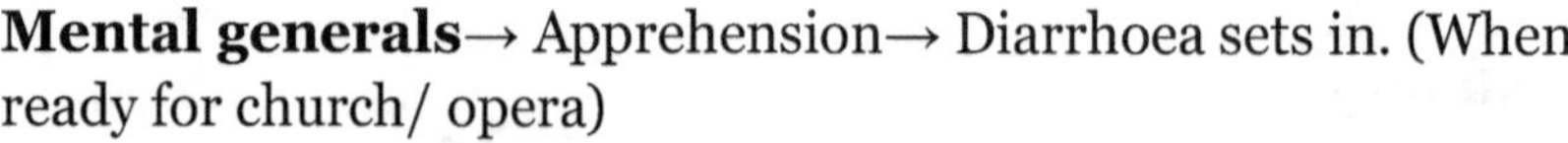

Hurry.

Must walk fast.

Anxious

Irritable & nervous.

Physical generals→ Acute/ chronic disease.

From→ unusual, long- continued mental exertion.

Emaciation. (marked in lower extremities)

Marasmus.

Desire→ for fresh air. (imp.)

Craves→ sugar, fresh air, wind blowing in his face.

Chilly→ when uncovered. (Feel smothered if wrapped up)

General modalities→ Agg.→ Cold foods, cold air.

Eating→ sugar, ice cream.

Unusual mental exertion.

Amel.→ Open air.

Craves→ wind blowing in his face.

Bathing→ cold water. (imp.)

Particulars→

Head→ Headache (imp.)

Sensation→ Congestive, fullness, heaviness,

Sense of expansion, pressive, screwing.

Site→ Habitual gastric, hemicrania, frontal eminence.

Ending→ Bilious vomiting.

Particular modalities→

<mental labour

<by pressure

Relief from→ tight bandaging.

Throat→

Sensation→ splinter in throat. (When swallowing)

Urinary system→

Urine pass unconsciously.

During→ day & night.

Male reproductive system→

Impotence.

Erection absent→ when coition attempted.

Respiratory system→

Chronic laryngitis of singers.

High notes→ causes cough.

Nervous system→

Walk, stands→ unsteadily. (when he thinks himself unobserved)

Convulsions→ great restlessness.

Trembling, can't walk eyes closed. (great weakness of lower extremity)

Female rep. System→

Sensation→ splinter like.

Site→ uterus.

When walking/ riding.

Coition painful both in female & male.

Bleeding from vagina.

Metrorrhagia→ in:

Young widows

Sterility

Nervous erethism at change of life.

Eyes→ Acute granular conjunctivitis.

Appearance→ scarlet red. (Like a raw beef)

Discharge→ mucopurulent.

Opthalmia neonatrum→ 200th or 1000th potency as a topical application.

Discharge→ Profuse & purulent.

Cornea→ opaque, ulcerated.

Lids→ sore, thick, swollen. (Agglutinated in the morning)

Eye strain from sewing. (<warm room, ameliorate by open air)

G.I.System→ Craves→ sugar.

Diarrhoea→ Result of eating sugar.

Belching accompanies most gastric ailments.

Flatulent dyspepsia.

Diarrhoea→ (imp.)

As soon as he drinks; green mucous.

Like chopped spinach in flakes.

Turning green on diaper.

After→ eating candy/ sugar & drinking.

Masses of mucolymph. (in shreddy particle)

Much noisy flatus.

ARNICA MONTANA

Common name→ Leopard's bane.

Family→ Compositae.

Constitution→ Nervous woman.

Sanguine plethoric persons.

Very red face.

Adapted to those→ who remains long impressed by→ slight mechanical injury.

Mental generals→

Unconsciousness→ when spoken to answer correctly.

Unconsciousness & delirium at once return.

Says→ there is nothing the matter with him.

Physical generals→

Sore, lame, bruised feeling all through body. (As if beaten)

Traumatic affection→ of muscle.

Nervous & over sensitive.

Everything on which he lies seems too hard.

Search a soft spot.

General modalities→ **Agg.**→ At rest.

Lying down.

From wine.

Amel.→ From contact.

Motion.

Particulars→

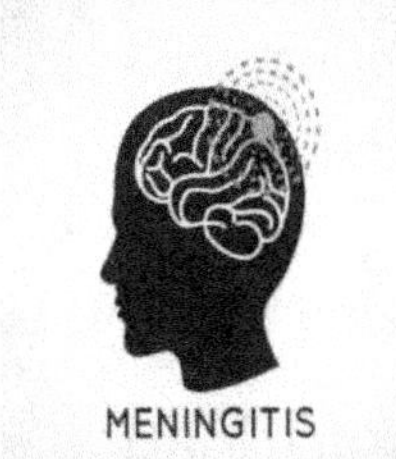

Head→ Hydrocephalus→ deathly coldness of forearm.

Meningitis→ after mechanical/ traumatic injuries

From fall

Concussion of brain.

Suspecting exudation to facilitate absorbtion.

Nervous system→ Mechanical injury→ concussion with stupor.

Involuntary feces& urine.

Apoplexy→ Loss of consciousness

Involuntary ejaculation of bladder and bowels.

Control→ hemorrhages

Acid absorption.

Paralysis→ Left- sided.

Pulse→ full, strong, stertor, sighing, muttering.

Female rep. System→ Soreness of parts→ after labor.

Prevent→ Post- partum hemorrhage &

Perperal complications.

After labor→ retention or incontinence of urine.

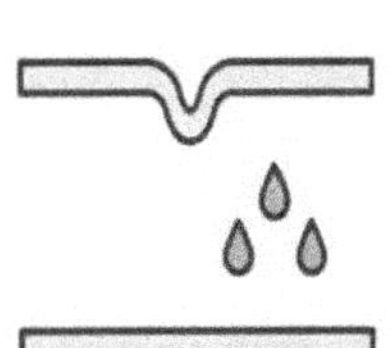

Extremities→ Gout & rheumatism.

Great fear of being touched or struck by persons

Can't walk erect on account of bruised sort of feeling,

Site→ pelvic region.

G.I.System→

Belching & eructation. (Foul, putrid, like rotten eggs)

Dysentery + ischuria.

Fruitless urging.

Long intervals between stools.

Constipation→ Rectum loaded.

Feces will not come away.

Ribbon- like stools. (From→ enlarged prostate or retroverted uterus)

Eyes→

Conjuctival & retinal haemorrhage.

(+) Extravasation.

Causes→ injury or cough.

Fever→ **(imp.)**

Heat of upper part of body. (Face + head)

Coldness of lower. (Remaining body)

Skin→ Tendecy:

Small boils→ painful

One after another

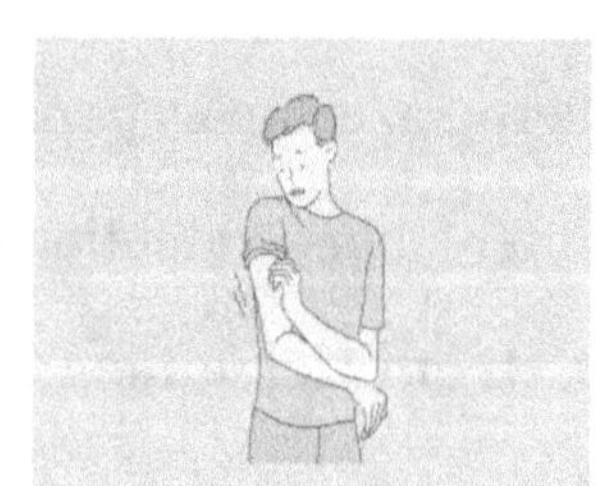

Extremely sore.

Injuries→ (imp.)

Bad effects of mechanical injury. (Even received years ago)

Blunt instrument injury.

Compound fracture. (Profuse supuration)

Concussion & contusion. (Results of→ shock or injury)

Prevent→ supuration & septic condition.

Promotes→ absorption.

ARSENICUM ALBUM

Common name→ White oxide of Arsenic.

Chemical formula→ As_2O_3

Mental generals→ (imp.)

Disposition :

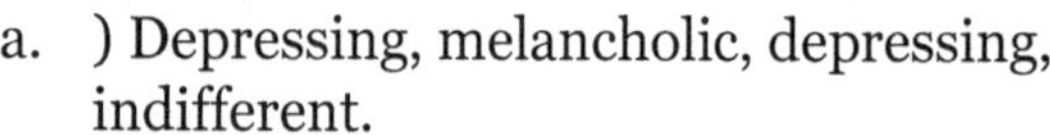

    a.) Depressing, melancholic, depressing, indifferent.
    b.) Anxious, fearful, restless, full of anguish.
    c.) Irritable, sensitive, peevish, easily vexed.

Greater suffering→ greater anguish.

Fear of death.

Think it useless to take medicine.

Is incurable condition.

Is surely going to die.

Dread of death. (alone)

Mentally restless but physically to weak to move. (imp.)

Change place continually.

Attacks of anxiety at night. (<after midnight)

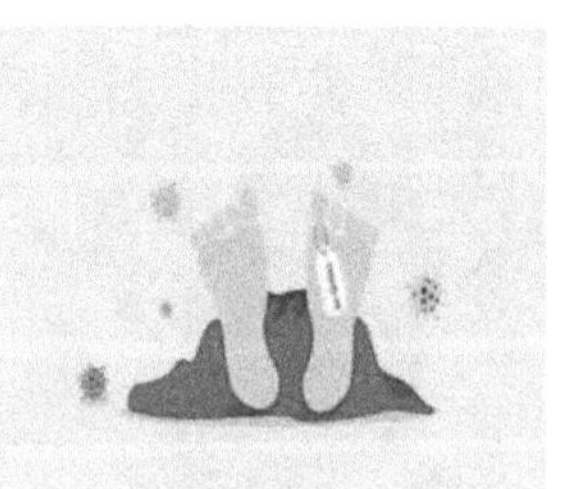

Teething children→ pale, weak, fretful.

Want to be carried rapidly.

Physical generals→ Great prostration. (Rapid sinking of vital forces)

Burning pains→ affected part burn like fire. (As hot coal application)

Particular modalities→ Ameliorate by: heat, hot drinks, hot application.

Can't bear smell or sight of food.

Great thirst. (Unquenchable for cold water)

Drinks→ often but little. (Sip- sip)

Eat→ seldom but much.

Rapid emaciation. Marasmus.

Exhaustion→ from little exertion.

General modalities.

Ailments→ bad effect from decayed food. (By inoculation, olfaction, or ingestion)

Complaints→ return annually.

General modalities→ **Agg.**→ After midnight (1 to 2 a.m. or p.m.)

From cold, cold drinks/ foods.

Lying on→ affected side. (Head low)

Amel.→ Heat in general.

Except→ Headache; ameliorated by cold bathing.

Particulars→ **Skin**→ Anasarca: skin pale, waxy, earth coloured

Dry, scaly, cold blue, wrinkled

Cold, clammy perspiration. (Like parchment)

White and pasty

Black vesicles and burning pain.

Respiratory system→ (must sit or bend forward)

Breathing asthmatic.

After→ 12 o'clock. Attacks like croup.

Unable to lie down to fear of suffocation.

SHORTNESS OF BREATH

G.I.System→ Burning thirst without desire.

Because→ stomach not seem to tolerate. (Because can't assimilate)

Cold water→ lies→ like a stone in stomach.

Wanted but not dare to drink.

Gastric derangements→

Cause→ after cold fruits, ice cream, ice water, sour bear

Bad sausage, alcoholic drinks, strong cheese.

Diarrhoea→ After eating or drinking.

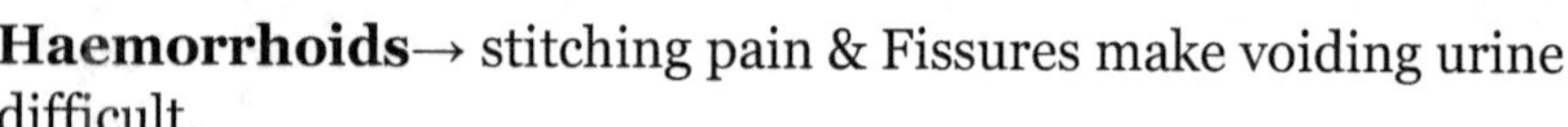

Stool→ scanty, dark- coloured.

Followed by→ great prostration.

Haemorrhoids→ stitching pain & Fissures make voiding urine difficult.

During→ walking or sitting.

Preventing sleep.

AURUM TRIPHYLLUM

Common name→ Indian turnip.

Family→ Araceae.

Physical generals→ Children:

Refuse food and drink. (Due to soreness of mouth)

Sleepless.

Face→

Patient pic & bore→ raw bleeding surfaces.

Painful→ but keep boring.

Pic lips until they bleed.

Corners of mouth→ sore, cracked, bleeding.

Bites nails→ fingers bleed.

Sour mouth & nose→ In malignant scarlatina & diphtheria.

Nose→ (imp.) Sym. of cold

Coryza→ Acrid, fluent, nostrils raw.

Nose feel stopped. (Sneezing; <at night)

Discharge→ acrid, ichorous.

Excoriating inside of nose, alae, upper lip.

Constant picking at nose→ until it bleeds.

Mouth→

Saliva profuse.

Acrid.

Corodes mucous membrane.

Tongue & buccal cavity→ raw & bleeding.

Throat→ (imp.)

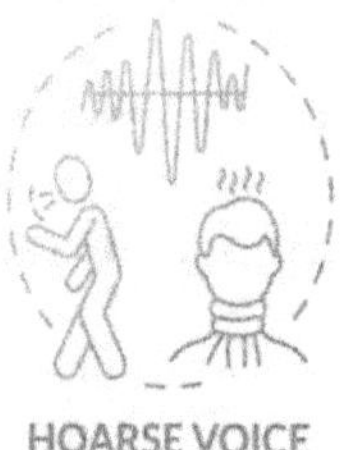

Voice hoarse.

Aphonia→ cause: from singing

After exposure to north- west winds.

Clergyman's sore throat→

In orator, singer, actor.

<talking, speaking, singing.

Fever→

Typhoid scarlatina.

Apathy, scanty or suppressed urine.

Threatened uremia.

Skin→

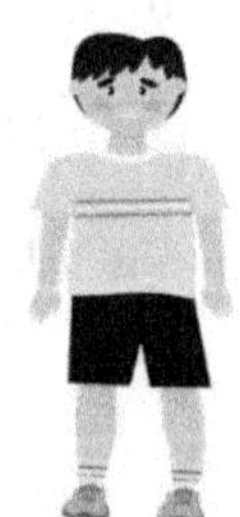

Desquamation. (In large flakes)

Second/ third time in scarlatina.

BAPTISIA TINCTORIA

Common name→ Wild indigo.

Family→ Leguminoseae.

Constitution→ Lymphatic temperament.

Mental generals→ Aversion to mental exertion.

Indisposed.

Perfect indifference.

Doesn't care to do anything.

Inability to fix mind on work.

Can't go to sleep because she can't get herself together. (Head or body feels scattered)

Stupor→ Falls asleep while being spoken&

Midst of his answer.

Physical generals→ Great prostration.

Whatever position patient lies, the part rested upon feel sore, lame & bruised.

Disposition→ to decomposition of fluids.

Ulceration of mucous membrane.

All discharge fetid→

Ex. Breath, stool, urine, perspiration, ulcers etc.

(Especially in typhoid & other acute disease)

Face→

Flushed.

Dusky.

Dark red.

Stupid, besotted, drunken expression.

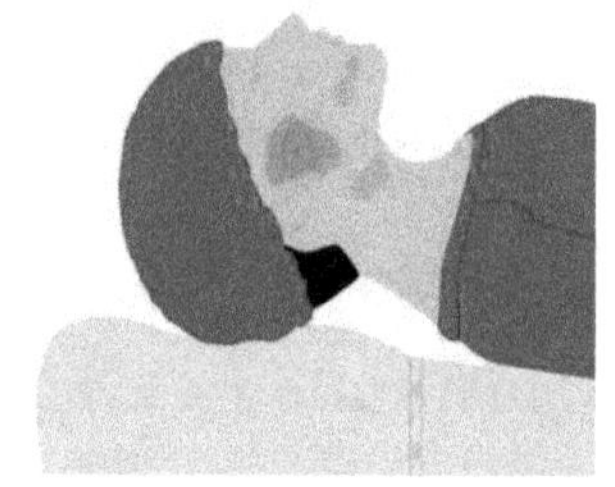

Fever→ (imp.)

Decubitis. (In typhoid)

Discharge→ fetid.

Throat→ (imp.)

Can swallow liquid only

Least solid food gags.

Painless sore throat, tonsils. (imp.)

Soft plate and parotids→ dark red, swollen, putrid.

Offensive discharge.

Mouth→

Tongue→ First: coated + red papillae.

Dry & yellow brown in centre.

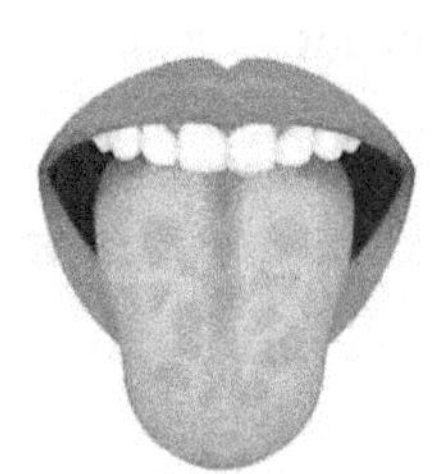

Later: dry, cracked & ulcerated.

G.I.System→

Dysentery→ in old people.

Diarrhoea→ in children. (When very offensive

BELLIS PERENNIS

Common Name→ Daisy / Day's eye

Family→ Compositae

Mental generals→

Resilient type of person (Person comes in normal stage after some time)

Impulsive to move

Patient usually wakes up at 3 A.M. and cannot get to sleep again

Physical generals→

Over worked old labours and workmen (Stretching of muscles)

Itching on back and flexor surfaces of thigh

Wrist feels contracted as from elastic band around joint

Railway spine

'Stasis & fag' – Swellings of all kinds, varicose veins, engorgement of breast and uterus, cerebral stasis etc.

Traumatism of pelvic organs with sore, burnished feeling in pelvic region.

General modalities→ **Agg.**→ Worse after hot bath & warm of bed before storms,

getting cold after over heated.

Amel.→ By local cold pressure.

Particulars→

Injuries→

OPERATION – Keloid after surgical injuries

VENOUS STARIES – Trauma at veins

PREGNENCY & CHILD BIRTH – Injury during pregnency

RAILWAY SPINE – Injuries in spine while travelling

NERVOUS INJURY – Deep nervous injury

Head→

Vertigo in elderly people

Headache from occiput to top of head

Forehead feels contracted

Itching around scalp and over back

Skin→

Small boils (very sensitive to touch) at lower jaw (after chewing of flowers) and large boils on back of neck, commencing with a dull, aching pain.

Vesicular like paches and eruptions are sore.

Female rep. System→

Amenorrhoea (No menses)

Breasts and uterus engorged

Varicose veins in pregnancy

Uterus feels sore as if squeezed.

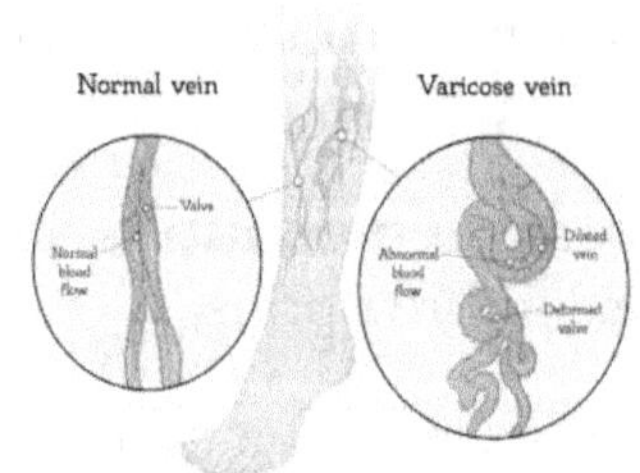

BRYONIA ALBA

Common name→ White bryony or Wild hop.

Family→ Cucurbitaceae.

Constitution→ Rheumatic or gouty diathesis persons.

Prone to so-called bilious attacks.

Dark/black hair, dark complexion, firm muscle fibre.

Bryonia patient→ Irritable.

Inclined to be vehement & angry.

Nervous, slender people.

Mental generals→

Ailments→ chagrin, mortification, anger, violence.

(with chilliness and coldness)

After anger chilly + (Hed hot and face red)

Delirium→ Business minded

Desire to get out of bed and go home.

Desire things immediately→ when offered→ refused.

Children dislike to be caried or raised.

Physical generals→

Complaints→ when warm weather sets in after cold days.

After taking cold or getting hot in summer.

Kicks the covers off.

Exposure to: drafts, cold wind,

suppressed discharge.(i.e. menses, milk, eruption of acute exanthema)

Pains→ type: stitching,

tearing. (Worse at night)

Gen. Modalities.

Excessive dryness of mucous membrane of entire body.

Lips & tongue (dry + perched)

Urine→ dark + scanty.

Great thirst→ for large quantities at long intervals. (imp.)

General modalities→ **Agg.**→ Motion, exertion, touch.

Warm, warm food, suppressed discharge.

Amel.→ Lying (especially→ on painful side)

Pressure, rest,eating cold things.

Particulars→

Head→ **(imp.)** Headache (in morning after rising)

Cause→ stooping, ironing, coughing.

Sensation→ Brain would burst through forehead.

From constipation.

Respiratory system→ Cough→ Dry, spasmodic.

(+ gagging & vomiting)

(+ stiches in side of chest)

(+ headache; as fly to pieces)

Particular modality→ After:

< eating or drinking.

< entering a warm room.

< deep inspiration.

Extremities→

Constant motion of left arm & leg.

Female rep. System→ (imp.)

Mastitis→ mammae heavy. (Stony hardness)

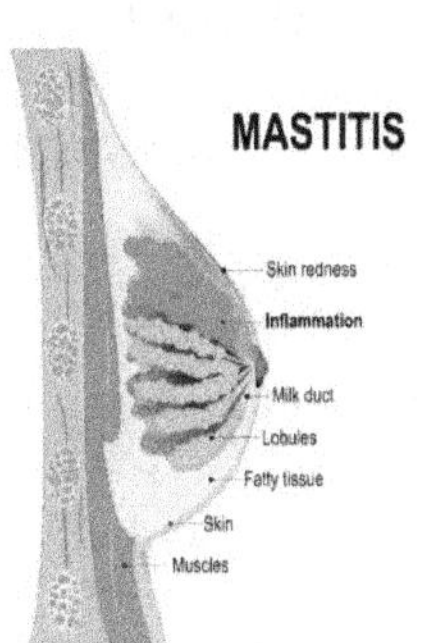

Pale but hard.

Hot + painful.

Support→ breast.

Vicarious menstruation→ nosebleed,

Blood spitting & haemoptysis.

G.I.system→ (Pressure as stone in the stomach)

Patient can't sit from nausea & faintness.

Constipation→ inactive, no inclination.

Stool→ large, hard, dark, burnt, dry.

(On going to sea)

Diarrhoea→ (morning + moving)

Of undigested food.

CALCAREA FLUORICA

Common name→ Calcium fluoride / Fluor spar.

Chemical formula→ CaF_2

Mentalgenerals→

Depression→ marked & groundless fears of financial ruin.

Sleep: Vivid dreams, with sense of impending danger. Unrefreshing sleep.

General modalities→ **Agg.**→ during rest & changing weather.

Amel.→ from heat & warm applications.

Particulars→

Head→ Creaking noise in head.

Blood-tumors (new-born infants)

Hard excrescences & ulcers on scalp.

Cataract

Eyes→ Flickering & sparks before the eyes,

spots on the cornea & conjunctivitis.

cataract.

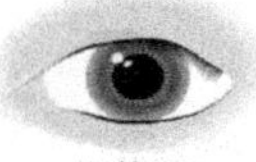

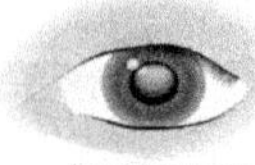

Ears→ Calcareous deposits on tympanum.

Sclerosis of ossicula and petrous portion of temporal bone.

Associated symptoms→ deafness, ringing and roaring.

Chronic suppuration of middle ear.

Nose→ Cold in the head, dry coryza, ozaena.

Nasal catarrh→ Copious, offensive, thick, greenish, lumpy, yellow.

Atrophic rhinitis. (Especially if crusts→ prominent)

Face→ Hard swelling on the cheek.

Toothache & hard swelling on jaw.

Mouth→ Gum-boil, with hard swelling on the jaw.

Tongue→ Cracked; induration & hardening.

Throat→ Follicular sore throat.

Pain and burning in throat.

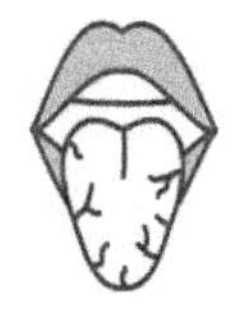

Better by→ warm drinks; worse, cold drinks.

Hypertrophy of Luschka's tonsil.

G.I.System→ Vomiting of infants. (Of undigested food)

Hiccough& much Flatulency.

Weakness and daintiness of appetite.

Acute indigestion from fatigue and brain-fag.

Diarrhoea: in gouty subjects.

Itching of anus.

Fissure of the anus & sore crack near lower bowel.

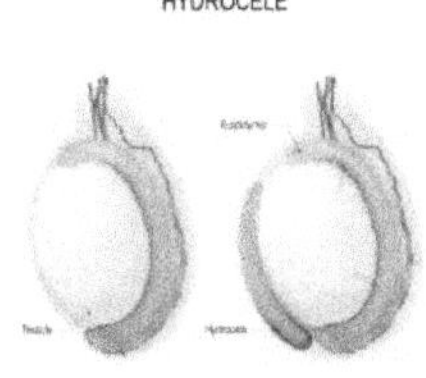

Bleeding haemorrhoids. (Internal piles)

Itching of anus as from pin-worms.

Constipation.

Male rep. System→ Hydrocele & indurations of testicles.

Respiratory system→ Hoarseness.

Croup, Spasmodic cough.

Expectoration of tiny lumps of yellow mucus.

Sensation→ Tickling and irritation on lying down.

Circulatory Organs→ Chief remedy for vascular tumour.

Extremities→ Ganglia or encysted tumors at the back ofwrist.

Gouty enlargements→ of joints of the fingers.

Fingers exostoses.

Chronic synovitis of knee-joint.

Skin→ Marked whiteness of skin. Scar tissue

Adhesions after operations.

Chaps and cracks.

Stony hardness and induration of gland.

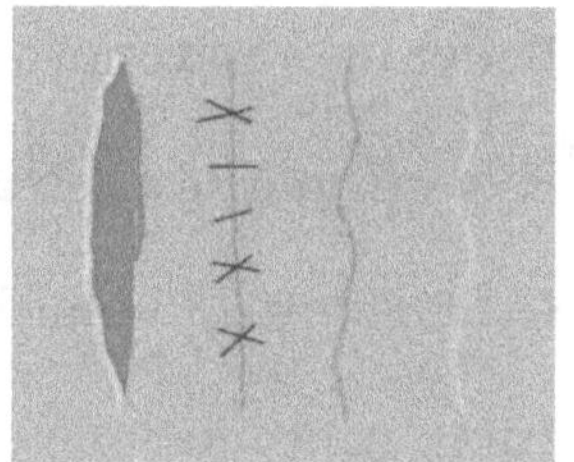

CALCAREA OSTREARUM

Common name→ Middle layer of oyster shells.

Chemical formula→ $CaCO_3$

Constitution→ Leucophlegmatic.

Blonde hair, light complexion, blue eyes.

Fair skin, obese youth.

Psoric constitution→ pale, weak, timid & easily tired.

Disposed→ to grow fat, corpulent, unwieldy.

Children→ Red face, flaby muscle.

Sweat easily, take cold readily.

Large hands + abdomen.

Fontanelles & sutures open.

Bone→ soft; develop→ slowly.

Girls→ Fleshy, plethoric; grow→ rapidly.

Difficult & delayed→ dentition.

Mental generals→ Fears.

She will lose her reason.

People will observe her mental confusion.

Physical generals→

Profuse perspiration. (On back, head & neck, chest)

Sweat→ of single parts. (Head, chest, sexual organ, hand, scalp, feet etc.)

Great longing→ for eggs, fresh air.

Aversion→ meat, cold open air.

Great liability to take cold.

Desire→ to be magnatised.

Disease→ due to: **(ailments)**

Defective assimilation.

Imperfect ossification.

Difficulty→ in walk & standing&

Suppressed sweat.

Uremic & other diseases→ From:

Standing in cold, damp pavements.

Modelers/ workers in a cold clay.

Extremity→ crooked, deformed & irregularly developed.

General modalities→ **Agg.**→ Cold air, wet weather, Cold water, washing, morning, during full moon.

Amel.→ Dry weather, lying on painful side.

Particulars→

Head→ Sweat profuse.

While sleeping.

Wetting pillow far around.

Extremity→

Rawness→ soles of feet.

Perspiration→ offensive.

Blisters.

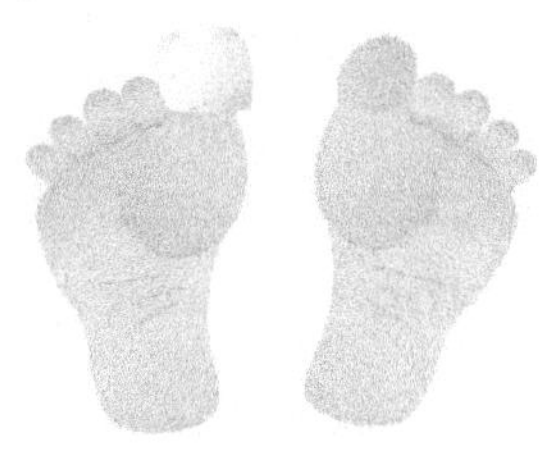

Respiratory system→

Lung disease.

Site→ upper third of the right lung.

Guide→ constitutional remedy.

Painless hoarsness. (< in morning)

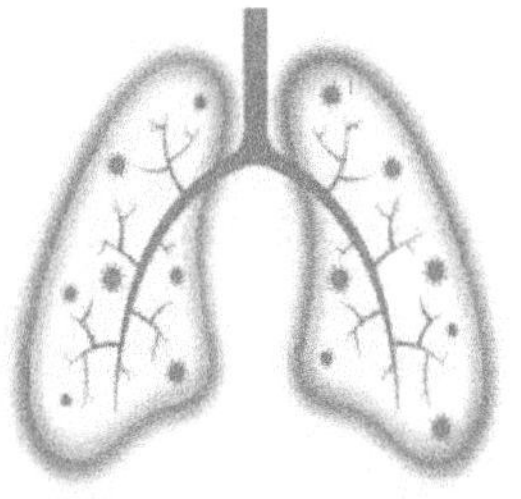

Female rep. System→ Menstruation:

Too early, too profuse, too long lasting.

Menses→ scanty, suppressed.

Amenorrhoea + chlorosis.

Cold damp stockings. (Feet)

Least mental excitement→ return of menstrual flow.

G.I.System→ Acidity of digestive tract.

Sour eractation & vomiting.

Sour stool & odour.

Pit of stomach→ swollen. (Like inverted saucer)

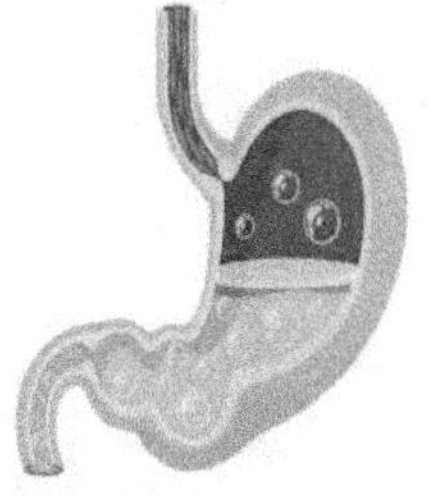

Painful to pressure.

Stool removed→ mechanically.

Constipation→ feels better in every way.

CALCAREA PHOSPORICA

Common name→ Phosphate of lime.

Chemical formula→ $Ca_3(PO_4)_2$

Constitution→ **(imp.)** Anemic persons.

Dark complexion. Dark hair & eyes.

Thin→ subject. (Instead of fat)

Girls→ at puberty, tall, rapidly growing,

Tendency→ Bones→ soften; spine→ curvature.

Scorfulous children→ first & second dentition.

Diarrhoea + flatulence.

Children→ emaciated, unable to stand,

Slow in learning to walk, sunken, flabby (abdomen)

At puberty→ Acne (in anemic girls)

(+ vertex headaches & flatulence dyspepsia)

Ameliorated by→ eating.

Mental generals→

Ailments→ from grief, disappointed love.

Feels complaints more→ when thinking about them.

Involuntary sighing.

General modalities→ **Agg.**→ Damp, cold, changeable weather.

East wind, melting snow, mental exertion.

Amel.→ In summer, warm, dry atmosphere.

Particulars→ **Head**→

Rachitis→ cranial bone thin & brittle.

Fontanelles and sutures remain open too long. (Close and reopen)

Delayed teething.

Headache of school girls. (Diarrhoea)

Non-union of bones. (Promotes→ callous)

Back and extremities→

Spine weak.

Disposed→ spine to curvature. (Unable to support body)

Especially→ left.

Neck weak→ unable to support head.

Rheumatism→ in cold weather.

Getting well→ in spring.

Return→ in autumn.

G.I.System→ Diarrhoea.

Oozing of body fluids. (From→ navel of infants)

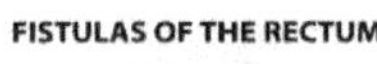

Colicky pain in abdomen. (At every attempt to eat)

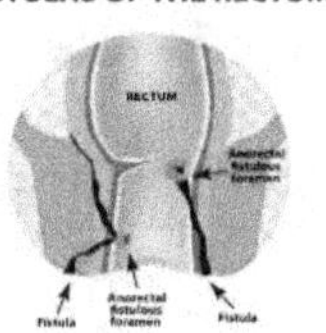

Fistula in ano (alternate with chest symptoms)

With general coldness of body.

CALCAREA SULPHURICA

Common name→ Gypsum; plaster of Paris; sulphate of calcium.

Chemical formula→$CaSO_4$

Particulars→ **Head**→

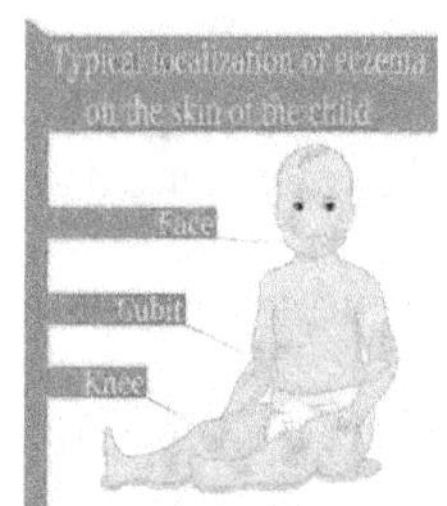

Scald-head of children. (purulent discharge)

Yellow, purulent crusts.

Eyes→ Ophthalmia neonatorum.

Inflammation of eyes & smoky cornea.

Discharge→ thick, yellow matter.

Sees only one-half of an object.

Ears→ Deafness:

Discharge of matter from middle ear. (Sometimes bloody)

Pimples around ear.

Face→ Herpes.

Pimples and pustules on the face.

Mouth→ Inside of lips sore.

Tongue→ flabby, resembling a layer of dried clay.

Yellow coating at base.

Throat→ Last stage of ulcerated sore throat.

G.I.System→ Pain in stomach.

Stool: Purulent diarrhoea mixed with blood.

Diarrhoea after maple sugar& from change of weather.

Pus-like, slimy discharge from bowels.

Painful abscesses about the anus in cases of fistula.

Female rep. System→ Menses late, long-lasting.

Concomitant→ headache, twitching great weakness.

Respiratory system→ Cough

Puulent & sanious sputa and hectic fever.

Empyaema, pus in the lungs / pleural cavities.

Purulent, sanious expectoration.

Catarrh, with thick, lumpy, white-yellow / pus-like secretion.

Extremities→

Burning-itching of soles of feet.

Fever→

Hectic fever, caused by formation of pus.

Concomitant→ cough & burning in soles.

Eczema (skin condition)

eczema

Skin→ Dry eczema in children.

Cuts, wounds, bruises, etc.

Unhealthy, purulent discharging pus. (Don't heal readily)

Purulent exudations in or upon the skin. ,matterless pimples under hair→ bleeding.

Skin affections + yellowish scabs.

CALENDULA OFFICINALIS

Common name→ Marigold.

Family→ Compositae.

Skin→

Ulcers→ Irritable, inflammation, sloughing, varicose.

Painful→ as if beaten.

Excessive secretion→ of pus.

Injuries→ (imp.)

Specific→ Clean, surgical cut, lacerated wound.

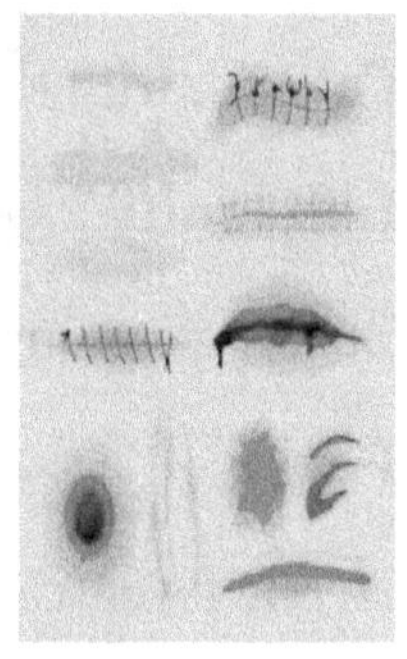

Traumatic injury.

Secure union by first intention.

All cases→ loss of soft parts.

(When adhesive plaster can't unite)

External wounds.

Torn or jagged wounds.

Post surgical operations.

Promote→ healthy granulations.

Prevent→ supuration.

Disfiguring scar.

Traumatic & idiopathic neuroma.

Neuritic→ by lacerated wound.

Loss of blood, excessive pain.

Rupture of muscle & tendon.

Laceration→ during labor.

Wound→ penetrating→ loss of synovial fluids.

Old neglected offensive, threatening gangrene.

Erysipelas.

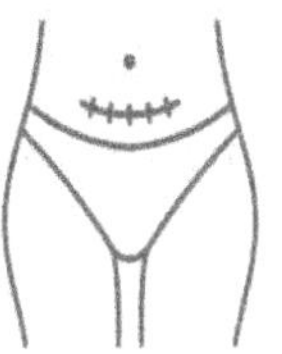

CHAMOMILLA

Common name→ Matricaria chamomilla.

Family→ Compositae.

Constitution→ Children, new- born.

Light brown hair.

Nervous excitable→ temperament.

Over sensitive→ use of coffee/ narcotics.

During period of dentition.

Mental generals→ Child:

Peevish, irritable, fretful.

Over sensitive→ to pain.

Driven→ to despair & snappish.

Can't return a civil answer.

Quiet→ only when carried.

Impatient, cross, spiteful.

Wants things become angry when refused.

Offered→ rejects it.

Too ugly to live.

Whining restlessness.

Averse to talk, answer peevishly.

Can't endure any one near him. (Cross)

Complaints→ from anger. (Chill & fever)

Physical generals→

Pains→ unendurable.

Drives to despair.

Numbness of affected part.

Over sensitive→ open air.

Aversion→ wind. (Especially about ears)

Sleepy but can't sleep.

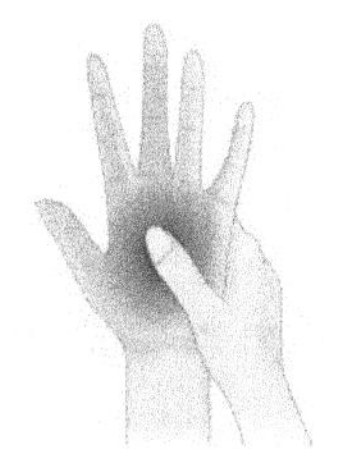

General modalities→ Agg.→ Heat, anger.

Evening, before midnight.

Open air, in the wind, eructations.

Amel.→ Being carried, fasting.

Warm, wet weather.

Particulars→

Mouth→ Toothache:

Cause→ anything warm taken into mouth.

On entering warm room.

In bed.

From→ coffee.

During→ menses & pregnancy.

Face→

One cheek (red & hot)

Other cheek (pale & cold)

Nervous system→

Convulsions of nursing children.

After→ a fit of anger in mother.

Female rep. System→ Labor pains:

Sensation→ spasmodic, distressing,

Tearing down legs, press upwards.

Nipples→ inflamed, tender to touch. (Also infant's breast)

Milk run out in→ nursing women.

G.I.System→

Diarrhoea (child bed) →cause:

Cold, anger, chagrin, after tobacco,

During dentition, downward motion.

Stool→ greeny, hot, watery.

Very offensive. (Like rotten eggs)

Corroding. (Like chopped egg or spinach)

CINA MARITIMA

Common name→ Worm seed.

Family→ Compositae.

Mental generals→ **(imp.)** Children:

Dark hair, very cross, ill humoured.

Want to be carried.

But carring giving no relief. (imp.)

Doesn't want to be touched.

Can't bear anyone near him.

Averse→ caresses.

Desire→ many things.

Rejects→ when offered.

Physical generals→

Canine hunger.

Hungry soon after full meal.

Craving→ sweets & different things.

Refuse→ mother's milk.

Particulars→

Nose→ Constant digging & boring at the nose.

Pick the nose all the time.

Itching→ of nose.

Rubs: on pillow or shoulder of nurse.

Face→ Pale & sickly.

White and blue appearance. (Around the mouth)

Dark rings→ under the eyes.

One cheek→ red.

Other cheek→ pale.

G.I.System→ Children:

Worm suffering. (imp.)

Pitiful weeping.

Awake→ start & screams during sleep.

Grinding of teeth. Ascarides.

Respiratory system→

Cough→ (Periodic- returning spring and fall)

Dry, sneezing, spasmodic, gagging.

In morning

Child→ Afraid to speak & move.

Due to fear of bringing cough.

Urinary system→ Urine:

Turbid→ when passed.

Milky& semisolid→ after standing.

White & turbid→ involuntary.

CINCHONA OFFICINALIS (CHINA)

Common name→ Peruvian bark/ china officinalis.

Family→ Rubiaceae

Constitution→ Stout & swarthy persons.

Once robust.

Become→ debilitated, broken down.

Due to→ exhausting discharges.

Mental generals→

Apathetic, indifferent, taciturn.

Despondent, gloomy, no desire to live.

Lack courage to commit suicide.

Physical generals→ Ailments→

Loss of vital fluids. (i.e. haemorrhage, excessive lactation, diarrhoea, supuration)

Malarial origin→ return every other day.

Disposition→ Haemorrhage,

From→ every orifice of the body. (Long continued)

Associated symptoms→ loss of sight, convulsion, fainting, coldness.

Pain→

Sensation→ drawing, tearing, sore, modalities.

Site→ every joints, bones, periosteum.

Move limb frequently.

Sleep→ unrefreshing/ constant spoor.

< 3a.m. & wakes early.

Haemorrhage→

Site→ mouth, nose, bowels, uterus.

Longing→ sour things.

General modalities→ Agg.→ Slightest touch, draft of air.

Every other day, mental emotion.

Loss of vital fluids.

Amel.→ Hard pressure, bending double.

Particulars→

Head→ Headache. (Must stand & walk)

Sensation→ as skull would burst.

Site→ from occiput→ to over whole head.

Particular modality→ <sitting.

<lying, after hemorrhage or sexual excess.

Face→ Pale & Hippocratic.

Eyes→ sunken, sickly expression,

Surrounded by blue margins.

Toothache→ while nursing child.

Female rep. System→ After climacteric.

Profuse haemorrhage.

Acute disease→ results dropsy.

Nervous system→ Great debility.

Trembling.

Aversion→ to exercise.

Sensitive→ (entire nervous system)

To touch, to cold, to drafts of air.

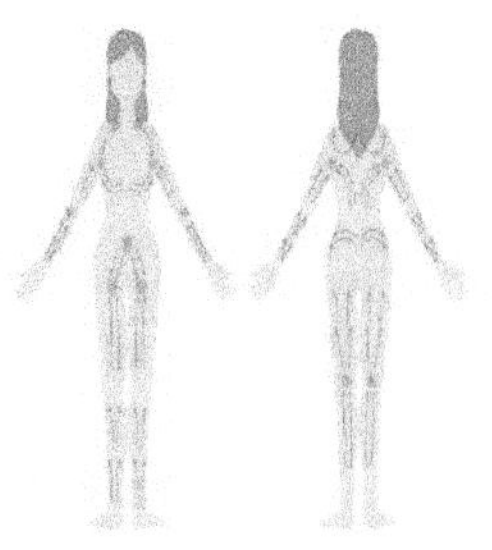

Extremities→

One hand→ icy cold.

Other→ warm.

Fever→ Intermittent.

Paroxysm→ 2-3hrs. each attack.

Returns→ 7/14 days. (Never at night)

Sweat profusely→ on being covered or during sleep.

G.I.System→ Excessive flatulence.

Fermentation & borborygmus.

Belching gives→ no relief.

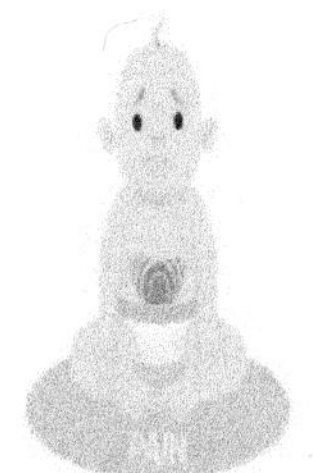

Colic→ at certain hour. (Each day)

Periodical.

From→ gall stones.

< at night, after eating.

Ameliorated by→ bending double.

COLCHICUM AUTUMNALE

Common name→ Meadow saffron.

Family→ Liliaceae.

Constitution→ Rheumatic, gouty diathesis.

Robust vigorous constitution.

Old people.

Mental generals→

Ailments: from grief & misdeeds of others.

External impression→ light, noise,

Strong odours, contact, bad manners.

Makes→ beside himself.

Sufferings→ seems intolerable.

Physical generals→

Pains→ drawing, tearing, pressing.

Light superficial pain→ in warm weather.

Bones, deeper tissue→ from cold air.

Shift→ left to right.

Bad effects of night watching.

Aversion→ food, loathing. (From sight or smell)

Affected part→ sensitive to contact & motion.

General modalities→ **Agg.**→ Mental emotion exhaustion.

Effect of hard study, odour of cooking food, motion.

If patient→ lies still→ disposition to vomit→ less urgent

But motion→ renews it.

Particulars→

Urinary system→ Urine:

Dark, scanty or suppressed, in drops.

White sediment, bloody brown, black, inky.

Clots of putrid decomposed blood + (albumin & sugar)

G.I.System→ Smell painfully acute.

Nausea & faintness from odour of cooking food.

Especially→ fish, eggs, or meat. (smell→ imp.)

Abdomen→ distended with gas, bursting feeling,

Burning & icy coldness.

Autumnal dysentery→ Discharge:

White shreddy particles (large quantities)

White mucous & scrapping of intestine.

Extremities→ Rheumatic complaint (imp.)

Arthritic pain.

Site→ joint.

Patient screams while touching a joint or stunning a toe.

(Due to→ pain)

COLOCYNTHIS

Common name→ Squirting cucumber.

Family→ Cucurbitaceae.

Mental generals→ (imp.)

Affection: colic, vomiting, diarrhoea, suppression of menses.

From→ anger& indignation.

Extremely irritable→ throw things out of hand.

Impatient.

Become angry/ offended on being questioned.

General modalities→ **Agg.**→Anger, indignation.

Mortification caused by offense.

Cheese. (Agg.→ colic)

Amel.→ From doubling up, hard pressure.

Particulars→

Head→ Vertigo:

Due to→ quickly turning head. (Esp.→ to left)

As he would fall from stimulants.

Extremities→ Sciatica:

Sensation→ crampy pain in hip, as screws in a wise.

Lies upon→ affected site.

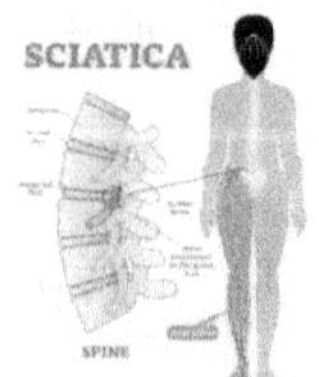

Shooting pain. (Like lightning shocks)

Down the whole limb→ left hip→ left thigh

→ left knee→ into popliteal fossa.

Female rep. System→

Menses; suppressed by→ chagrin.

Colic pains.

G.I.System→ (Colic→ imp.)

Agonizing pain.

Site→ abdomen.

Causing→ patient to bend double, restlessness,

Twisting, turning. (To obtain relief)

Ameliorated by→ hard pressure.

Pain→ < after eating, after drinking.

Compel→ patient to bend double.

DROSERA ROTUNDIFOLIA

Common name→ Sundew.

Family→ Droseraceae.

Particulars→

Throat→ Clergyman sore throat.

Rough, scrapping, dry sensation.

Deep in fauces.

Voice→ hoarse, deep, toneless.

Cracked, requires exertion to speak.

Respiratory system→ **(imp.)**

Whooping cough→ laryngeal pthisis. (Violent paroxysm)

Cough→ deep sounding, hoarse barking.

< after midnight.

During / after measles.

Concomitant→ gagging, retching, bleeding (nose & mouth)

Vomiting. (Water/ mucous)

Constant titillating cough in children.

Begin→ as soon as head touches pillow.

Nocturnal cough→ in young. (In pthisis)

Bloody / purulent sputa.

Cough modalities→ < by warmth, drinking, singing, laughing.

< by weeping, lying down, after midnight.

Sensation→ feather in larynx.

Exciting cough.

Disease prevailing→ epidemic disease.

Constriction & crawling→ in larynx.

Hoarseness + green sputa.

DULCAMARA

Common name→ Bitter- sweet.

Family→ Solanaceae.

Constitution→ Phlegmatic scorfulous Constitution.

Restless &irritable.

Patient living in / working in→ damp, cold basement ; milk dairy.

Mental generals→ Mental confusion.

Can't find right word for anything.

Physical generals→ Catarrhal rheumatism. (Skin affection)

General modalities.

Causation (imp.) → due to sudden changes in hot weather,

Suppressed discharge. (Sweat, menses)

Increased secretion of mucous membrane.

Perspiration→ suppressed from cold.

Anasarca→ after: ague, rheumatism, scarlet fever.

Dropsy→ after: suppressed sweat & eruption, exposure to cold.

General modalities→ **Agg.**→ Cold→ in general.

Cold air, cold wet weather.

Suppressed menstruation, eruption, sweat.

Amel.→ Moving about.

Particulars→

G.I.System→ Diarrhoea:

From→ taking cold. (In damp places)

Damp foggy weather.

Change from warm→ to cold weather.

Skin→ **(imp.)** Delicate.

Sensitive→ to cold.

Liable→ to eruptions. (Especially urticaria)

Causes→ patient takes cold / long exposed to cold.

Rash→ before menses.

Urticaria→ whole body. (No fever)

Itching burn due to scratching.

Aggravation→ in warmth.

Amelioration→ in cold.

Thick brown-yellow crust + reddish border. (Bleeding→ when scratched)

Site→ on scalp, face, forehead, temples, chin.

Warts→ flashy, large, smooth.

Site→ on face, back of hands & fingers.

EUPHRASIA OFFICINALIS

Common name→ Eyebright.

Family→ Scorphularaceae.

Physical generals→

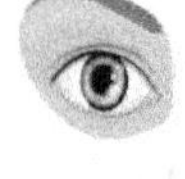

Bad effects from:

Fall, contusion or mechanical injury of ext. parts.

Catarrhal affection→ of mucous membrane.

Especially→ eyes, nose.

Eyes→ (imp.)

Profuse→ acrid lachrymation.

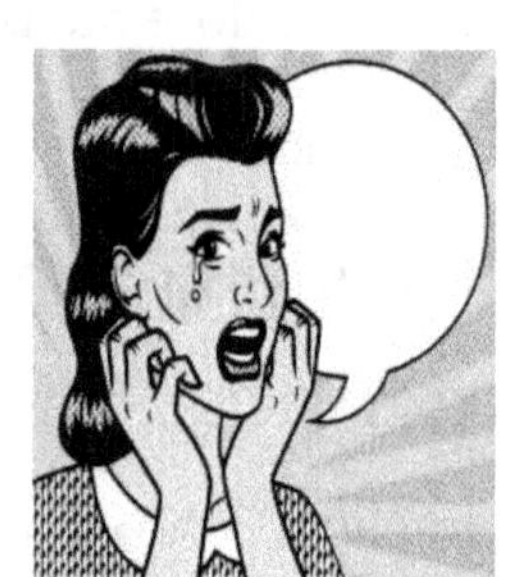

Profuse→ bland coryza.

Eyes water all the time.

Agglutinated in the morning.

Margins of lid→ red, swollen, burning.

Throat→

Attempts to clear throat.

Offensive mucous→ in morning.

Gagging until he vomits. (The breakfast just eaten)

Voluntary hawking→ profuse expectoration of mucus.

< on rising morning.

Pertussis→ increase lachrymation during cough.

Cough→ in day time.

Nose→

Profuse→ fluent coryza. (In morning)

Violent cough + abundant expectoration.

< warm South wind exposure.

Female rep. System→ Amenorrhoea:

Concomitant→ catarrhal symptoms. (Eyes & nose) &

Profuse acrid lachrymation.

Menses→ painful, regular,

Now lasting only 1hr. / late.

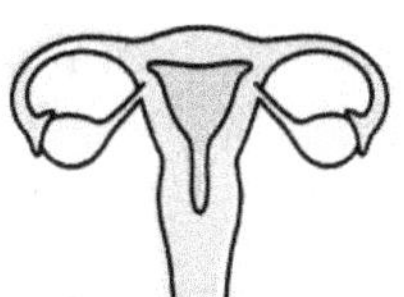

Scanty, short, lasting only one day.

FERRUM PHOSPHORICUM

Common name→ Ferroso-ferric phosphate.

Chemical formula→$FePO_4$

Constitution→

Grauvogl's Oxygenoid Constitution.

Typical Ferr phos subject is not full blooded & robust.

But nervous, sensitive, anaemic.

False plethora & easy flushing of Ferrum.

Prostration marked.

Mental generals→ Restless and sleepless.

Anxious dreams & Night sweats of anaemia.

Particulars→

Head→ Vertigo & headache.

Soreness to touch, cold, noise jar.

Sensation→ Throbbing & Rush of blood to head.

Ill effects of sun-heat.

Headache better cold applications.

Eyes→ Red, inflamed.

Sensation→ Burning & Feeling as sand under lids.

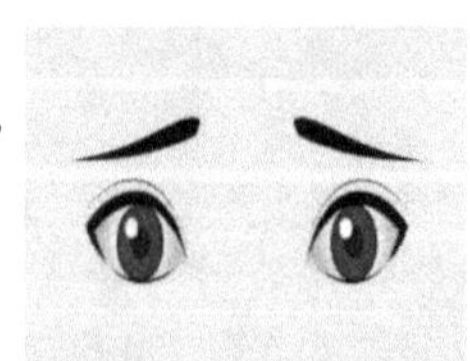

Hyperaemia of optic disc and retina.

Associated symptom→ blurred vision.

Ears→

Noises & Throbbing.

First stage of otitis. (Acute otitis)

Membrana tympani→ red & bulging.

Otitis

Face→

Flushed; cheeks sore &hot.

Florid complexion.

Facial neuralgia. (worse by→ shaking head and stooping)

Throat→

Mouth hot; fauces red, inflamed.

Ulcerated sore throat. Tonsils red and swollen.

Sore throat of singers.

Subacute laryngitis & First stage of diphtheria.

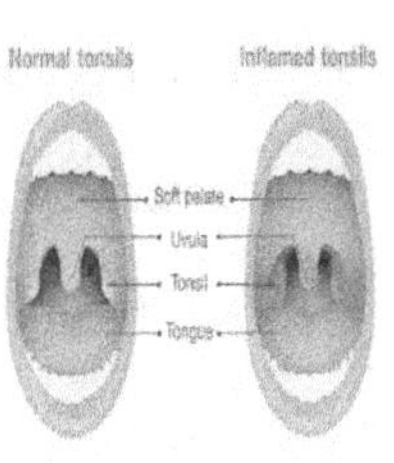

G.I.System→

Aversion→ meat and milk.

Desire→ for stimulants.

Vomiting of→ undigested food & bright red blood.

Sour eructations.

Haemorrhoids

First stage of peritonitis.

Stools→ watery, bloody, undigested.

PERITONITIS

First stage of dysentery, with much bloody discharges.

Urinarysystem→

Urine spurts with every cough.

Incontinence of urine. (Polyuria & Diurnal enuresis)

Irritation at→ neck of bladder.

Femalerep. System→

Menses every 3 weeks.

Bearing-down sensation & pain on top of head.

Vaginismus. Vagina dry & hot.

Respiratory system→

First stage of all inflammatory affections.

Congestions of lungs & haemoptysis.

Short, painful, dry, hard tickling cough. (Better at→ night)

Croup& sore chest.

Hoarseness & Epistaxis of nose.

Expectoration of pure blood in pneumonia.

Cardiovascular system→

Palpitation and pulse rapid.

First stage of cardiac diseases.

Short, quick, soft pulse.

Extremities→

Articular rheumatism.

Stiff neck & Crick in back.

Rheumatic pain in shoulder. (extend to→ chest and wrist)

Hands swollen and painful. (Palms hot)

Fever→ Chill daily at 1 pm.

All catarrhal and inflammatory fevers. (first stage)

GELSEMIUM SEMPERVIRENS

Common name→ Yellow jasmine.

Family→ Loganiaceae. (imp.)

Constitution→ Children, young people.

Women→ nervous hysterical temperament.

Excitable, irritable, sensitive.

Nervous affections of onanists of both male & female.

Mental generals→ **(imp.)**

Bad effects from fright, fear,

Exciting news & sudden emotions.

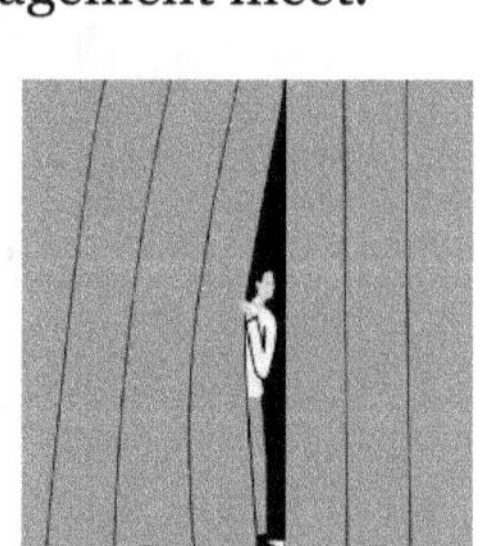

Fear of death.

Lack of courage.

Unusual ordeal preparing for church, theatre, engagement meet.

Bring→ coryza.

Stage fright, nervous.

Dread of appearing in public.

Desire to be quite, be alone.

Doesn't wish to speak.

Children→ fear of falling, grasp the crib or size the nurse.

Physical generals→

General depression. (Heat of sun/summer→ cause)

Weakness & trembling. (Tongue, hands, legs, entire body)

General modalities→ Agg.→ Damp weather, before thunderstorm.

Mental emotion, excitement, bad news.

Tobacco smoking, when thinking of his ailments.

When thinking of his loss.

Particulars→

Head→ Vertigo:

Spreading→ from occiput.

Associated symptoms→ diplopia, dim-vision, loss of sight.

Seems intoxicated→ when trying to move.

Headache:

Preceded→ blindness.

Ameliorated by→ profuse urination.

Begin→ in cervical spine.

Extend→ over head.

Sensation→ bursting.

Site→ forehead, eyes.

< mental exertion, modalities, lying head low.

Eyes→

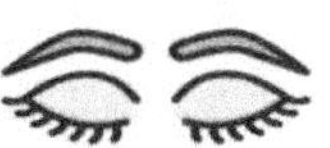

Great heaviness→ eyelids.

Can't keep them open.

Cardiovascular system→

Fear it would cease beating if she not moved.

Slow pulse→ of old age.

Nervous system→

Lack of muscular coordination.

Confuse, muscle refuse to obey the will.

Complete relaxation& prostration of whole muscular system + motor paralysis.

Fever→ (imp.)

Chill.

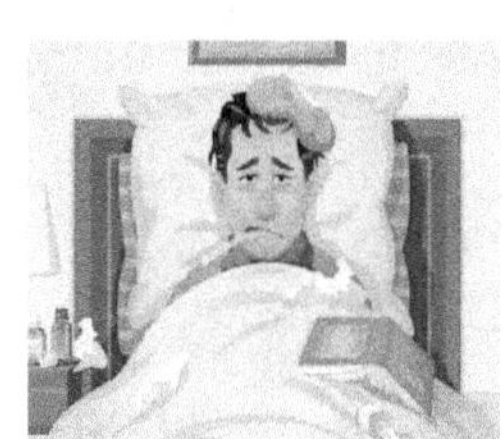

Thirst absent.

Along the spine.

Running up & down the back→ rapid.

From sacrum to occiput→ wave like succession.

HEPAR SULPHUR

Common name→ Sulphret of lime.

Chemical formula→ CaS

Constitution→ Torpid lymphatic Constitution.

Light hair & light complexion.

Slow to act.

Muscles→ soft, flabby.

Mental generals→ Quick.

Over sensitive. (Physically + mentally)

Slightest cause→ irritates.

Hasty speech & drinking.

Patient: peevish, angry→ least trifle,

Hypocondriachal, unreasonably anxious.

Physical generals→

Diseases→ due to abuse of mercury.

Extremely sensitive to cold air. (Feel the air of next room)

Wrapped up face. (Even in hot weather)

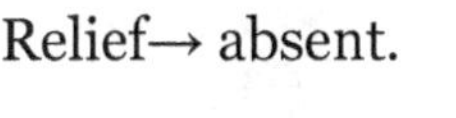

Takes cold. (Due to slightest exposure to fresh air)

Sweats→ profuse→ day & night.

Relief→ absent.

Perspiration→ sour, offensive,

Easily. (On mental or physical exertion)

General modalities→ **Agg.**→ Lying on→ painful side,

Cold air, uncovering, eating/ drinking cold things.

Touching affected part, mercury→ abuse.

Amel.→ warmth in general,

Wrapping up warmly. (Especially→ head)

In damp wet weather.

Particulars→

Eyes→

Eyeballs→ sour to touch.

Pain→ as they would be pulled back into head.

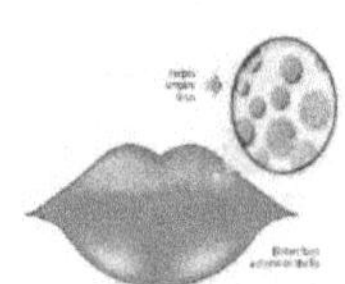

Face→

Middle of lower lip→ cracked.

Throat→ **(imp.)**

Sensation→ of splinter, fish bone, plug in throat.

Quinsy.

Supuration→ threatens.

Concomitant→ chronic hypertrophy, hardness of hearing.

Skin→ **(imp.)**

Slightest injury→ supuration.

Hepar→ open abscess.

Very sensitive to touch.

Can't bear even clothes to touch affected parts.

Pain causing fainting.

Skin affection→ extremely. (Ulcers & herpes)

Surrounded by→ little pimple or pustules.

Spread by→ coalescing.

Urinary system→ (imp.)

Urine: flow impeded.

Voided slowly. (Absent of force)

Drops vertically.

Before passing→ obligate to wait.

Bladder weak→ unable to finish.

Sensation→ as if some urine remains.

G.I.System→ Diarrhoea:

Children, clay coloured stool, sour smell.

Respiratory system→

Cough→

Croupy, chocking, strangling.

Deep, rough, barking.

Causation→ when any part of body is uncovered.

Exposure to: dry wet wind, dry cold wind, land wind.

Associated symptoms→ hoarseness, rattling of mucus.

Modalities→ < cold air, cold drinks.

< before midnight or towards morning.

Asthma→

Breathing→ anxious, wheezing, rattling.

Short & deep breathing.

Threatens suffocation.

Bend head back & sit-up. (Must)

After suppressed eruption→ asthma.

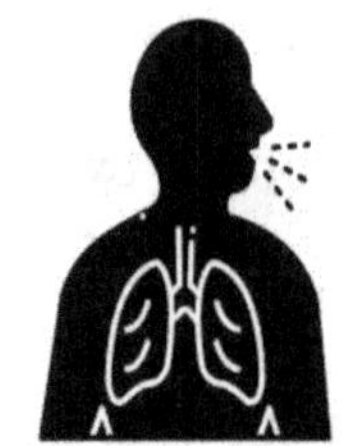

HYPERICUM PERFORATUM

Common name→ St. John's wart.

Family→ Hypericaceae.

Particulars→

Head→ Vertigo:

Sensation→ head become suddenly elongated. (At night)

Urging→ to urinate.

Headache:

After fall on occiput.

Sensation→ being lifted high into the air.

Great anxiety.

She fall from this height.

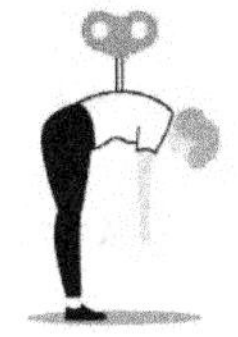

Extremities→

Bunions &corns.

Pain→ excruciating.

Showing→ nerve involvement.

Bunion in the foot

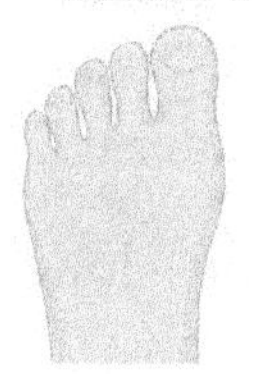

Back→

Spine→ very sensitive to touch.

After fall.

Slightest motion of arms or neck extorts cries.

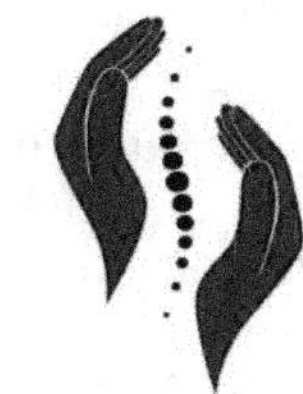

Nervous system→

Tetanus→ after traumatic injuries.

Nervous depression→ following: wounds & surgical wounds.

Removes→ bad effects of: shock, fright, mesmerism.

Convulsion→ after concussion,

Or blows on head.

Skin→ Always modifies.

Sometimes→ arrest ulceration, sloughing.

Crushed & mashed. (Fingertips)

Injuries→ Site→ fingers, toes, matrices of nails.

Palms or soles & Intolerable pain.

Mechanical injury→ spinal cord.

Bad effect of→ spinal concussion.

Pain→ after fall on coccyx.

Punctured, incised, lacerated wounds.

Especially of→ long duration.

Injury from→ treading on:

Nails, needles, pins, splinters, rat-bites.

Prevent→ lock jaw.

Preserve integrity of→ torn, lacerated wound.

When wound is almost separated from body.

Injury to parts→ sensitive in nerves.

IPECACUANHA

Common name→ Ipecac.

Family→ Rubiaceae.

Physical generals→

Disease with constant & continual nausea.

Haemorrhage→ active/ passive, bright red, (imp.)

From→ all the orifices of body.

Over sensitive→ to heat & cold.

Pains→ as bones were all torn to pieces.

General modalities→ **Agg.**→ Winter, dry weather.

< warm, moist, south winds, slightest motion.

Particulars→

G.I.System→

Adapted cases→ where gastric symptoms predominant.

Tongue→ clean, slightly coated.

Nausea + profuse saliva.

Vomiting→ white, glairy mucus in large quantities.

Sleepy afterwards.

< from stooping

Causes→ primary effect of tobacco, of pregnancy.

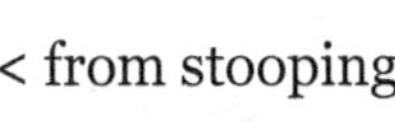

Stomach relaxed/ ameliorated by→ if hanging down,

Clutching, squeezing, griping (as from hand)

Each finger sharp pressing into intestines.

Worse from/ aggravation by→ motion.

Flatulent, cutting colic about umbilicus.

Stool→ grassy-green, white mucus, bloody,

Fermented, foamy, slimy, like frothy molasses.

Asiatic cholera→ nausea &vomiting predominant. (1st symptom)

Pain→ type: cutting.

Site→ across abdomen.

Move→ from left to right.

Autumnal dysentery→ cold nights, after hot days.

Intermittent dyspepsia→

Every other day. (At same hour)

Fever + persistent nausea.

Female rep. System→

Hemorrhage→ active or passive, bright red.

From→ uterus. (Profuse & clotted)

During→ stitches from naval to uterus.

Heavy, oppressed breathing.

Respiratory system→ (imp.)

Cough→ dry spasmodic, constricted, asthmatic.

Rattling of mucus in bronchi→ during inspiration.

Threatened suffocation. (From→ mucus)

Violent dyspnea + wheezing & anxiety. (About stomach)

Whooping cough.

Child lose breath→ turns pale, stiff & blue.

Associated symptoms→ Strangling, gagging & vomiting of mucus

Bleeding from nose & mouth.

Least exercise→ cause difficult breathing.

Fever→

Intermittent fever. (Beginning of→ irregular cases)

Associated symptoms→ nausea, gastric disturbance.

Causation/ailments→ after abuse of

Or suppression from→ quinine

.

KALIUM MURIATICUM

Common name→ Potassium chloride.

Chemical formula→ KCl

General modalities→

Agg.→ from rich food, fats, motion.

Particulars→

Head→ Headache + vomiting.

Crusta lactea & Dandruff.

Imaging→ starved.

Eyes→ Superficial ulcer & Trachoma.

Opacity of cornea.

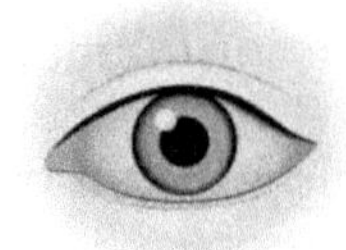

White mucus, purulent scabs

Ears→

Ear glands→ swollen.

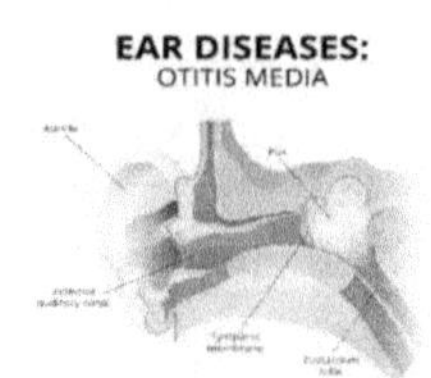

Chronic, catarrhal conditions of middle ear.

Noises in the ear.

Threatened mastoid, great effusion about auricle.

Face→ Cheek swollen & painful.

Mouth→ Aphthae, white ulcers in mouth.

Swollen glands→ about jaw and neck.

Tongue→ Coating of grayish-white, dryish, or slimy.

Throat→ Follicular tonsillitis.

"Hospital" sore throat.

Tonsils inflamed; enlarged.

G.I.System→

Indigestion cause→ Fatty or rich food.

Vomiting→ of white, opaque mucus; water in the mouth.

Associated symptoms→ Pain in stomach +constipation.

Abdominal swelling & tenderness.

Flatulence.

Itching at anus. (Cause→ Thread-worm)

Constipation. (Stool→ light-colored)

Diarrhoea. (After→ fatty food)

Stools→ clay-colored, white, or slimy.

Dysentery & bleeding haemorrhoids.

Femalerep. System→

Menstruation→ too late / suppressed, checked / too early.

Discharge→ excessive dark-clotted, tough, like tar.

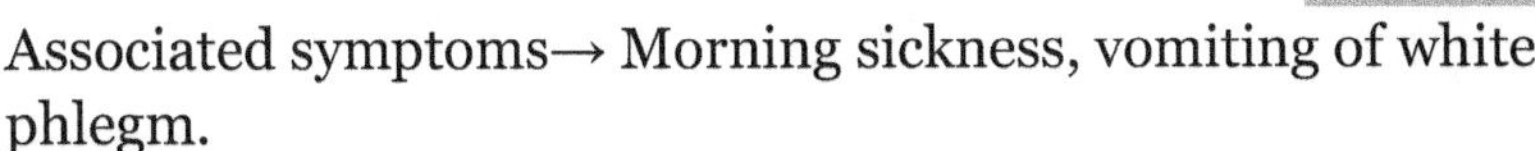

Leucorrhoea. (Discharge→ thick milky white)

Associated symptoms→ Morning sickness, vomiting of white phlegm.

Bunches in breast feel quite soft & tender.

Respiratory system→

Loss of voice, hoarseness.

Asthma, with gastric derangements.

Mucus→ hard & white.

Whooping-cough. (Expectoration→ thick and white)

Rattling sounds of breathing.

Difficult to cough up & catarrh.

Extremities→ Rheumatic fever,

Exudation & swelling around the joints.

Rheumatic pains aggravated→ night, during motion, warmth of bed.

Must get out of bed and sit up.

Sensation→ lightning-like from small of back to feet.

Hands get stiff while writing.

Skin→ Bursitis.

Acne, erythema & eczema.

Vesicles containing→ thick, white contents.

Dry, flour-like scales on skin.

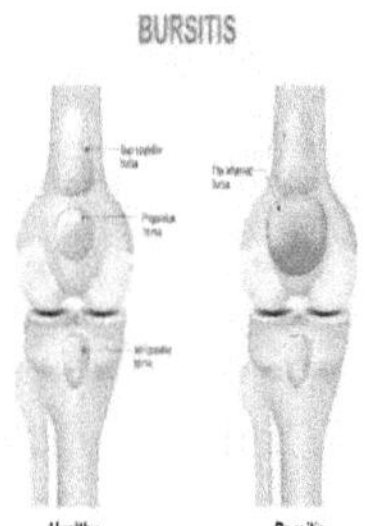

KALIUM PHOSPHORICUM

Common name→ Phosphate of potassium, potasse.

Chemical formula→K_3PO_4

Constitution→ Prostration, Weak & tired.

One of the greatest nerve remedies.

Adapted to the young. (Especially)

Marked disturbance→ of sympathetic nervous system.

Mental generals→

Anxiety, nervous dread, lethargy.

Indisposition to meet people, lassitude & depression.

Very nervous, easily irritable.

Brain-fag; hysteria; night terrors.

Loss of memory. Slightest lab or seems a heavy task.

Despondency about business. (Marked)

Shyness & disinclined to converse.

General modalities→

Agg.→ excitement, worry, mental & physical exertion;

eating, cold, early morning.

Amel.→ warmth, rest, nourishment.

Particulars→

Head→ Occipital headache

Better→ after rising.

Vertigo. (From→ lying, on standing up, sitting, when looking upward)

Cerebral anaemia.

Headache of students.

Headaches ameliorated→ by gentle motion.

Concomitant→ weary, empty, gone feeling at stomach.

Eyes→

Weakness of sight, perceptive power loss.

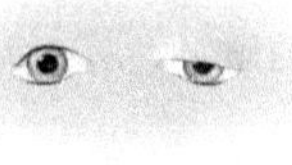

Causation→ after diphtheria; from exhaustion.

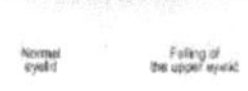

Drooping eyelids.

Ears→ Humming and buzzing in the ears.

Face→

Livid & sunken, with hollow eyes.

Right-sided neuralgia (Relieved by→ cold applications)

Mouth→

Breath offensive.

Tongue→ coated brownish, like mustard, dry in the morning.

Toothache, bleeding gums.

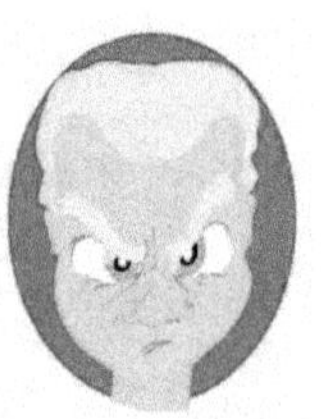

Gums spongy & receding.

Throat→ Gangrenous sore throat.

Vocal cords paralysis.

G.I.System→

Sensation→ nervous "gone" sensation at the pit of the stomach, seasick without nausea.

Diarrhoea. (Foul→ odour) (While→ eating)

Occasioned by→ fright, depression & exhaustion.

Dysentery. (Stools→ consist of pure blood)

Patient→ delirious & abdomen swells.

Cholera; stools have appearance of rice water.

Female rep. System→

Menstruation too late or too scanty.

In→ pale, irritable, sensitive & lachrymose females.

Discharge→ Too profuse, deep-red or blackish-red,

thin & not coagulating. (Odour→ offensive)

Feeble & ineffectual labor pains.

Male rep. System→

Nocturnal emissions.

Sexual power diminished utter prostration after coitus.

Urinary system→

Enuresis & Incontinence of urine.

Bleeding from→ urethra.

Colour of urine→ dark yellow.

Respiratory system→

Asthma. (Aggravates→ least food, going upstairs)

Cough. (Yellow expectoration)

Nasal disease + offensive discharge.

Fever→ Subnormal temperature.

Extremities→

Paralytic lameness in back & extremities.

Pains. (Aggravated by→ exertion)

Concomitant→ depression & subsequent exhaustion.

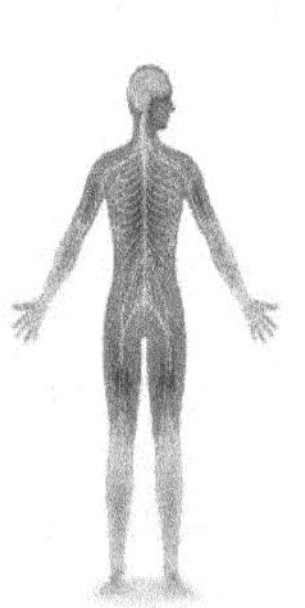

KALIUM SULPHURICUM

Common name→ Potassium sulphate.

Chemical formula→K_2SO_4

Physical generals→

Ailments accompanied by profuse desquamation.

Applicable to→ later stages of inflammation.

Dread→ of hot drinks.

Tongue→ coated yellow & slimy.

Smell→ lost.

General modalities→ **Agg.**→ in evening & heated room.

Amel.→ in cool & open air.

Particulars→

Head→ Rheumatic headache.

Beginning→ in evening.

Bald spots. (Dandruff & scaldhead)

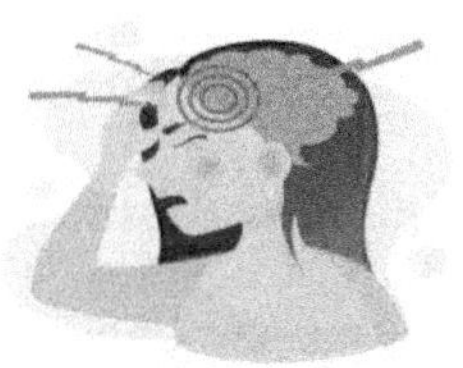

Ears→ Eustachian deafness.

Discharge→ yellow matter.

Face→ Epithelioma.

Aches→ in heated room.

G.I.System→

Nausea & vomiting.

Taste→ Insipid, pappy.

Colicky pains→ in abdomen.

Sensation in abdomen→ cold to touch, tympanitic, tense.

Diarrhoea→ Yellow, slimy.

Constipation with haemorrhoids.

Inflammation of the testes

Male rep. System→ Gonorrhoea & Orchitis.

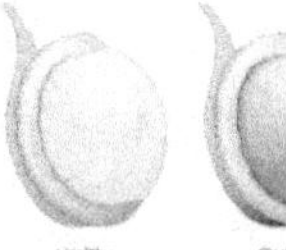

Discharge→ slimy, yellowish-green.

Female rep. System→

Menses too late, scanty & Metrorrhagia.

Sensation→ of weight in abdomen.

Respiratory system→ Coarse rales.

Rattling of mucus in chest.

Bronchial asthma. (Expectoration→ yellow)

Cough in children. (< in evening and in hot atmosphere)

Croupy hoarseness.

Cold. (Expectoration→ yellow & slimy)

Extremities→

Pain in nape, back& limbs. (Type→ shifting)

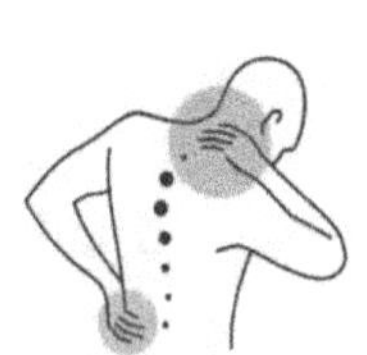

Aggravation→ in warm room.

Fever→

Intermittent fever. (Tongue→ yellow & slimy)

Rise of temperature at night

Skin→ Psoriasis & Eczema.

Eruption→ burning, itching, papular. (Nettle-rash)

Polyps; Epithelioma; Seborrhoea; Favus.

Ring-worm of scalp or beard with abundant scales.

LEDUM PALUSTRE

Common name→ Marsh tea.

Family→ Ericaceae.

Constitution→ Rheumatic, gouty diathesis.

Constitution→ abused by alcohol.

Complaints of→ people who cold all the time,

Always feel→ cold & chilly.

Lack of animal / vital heat.

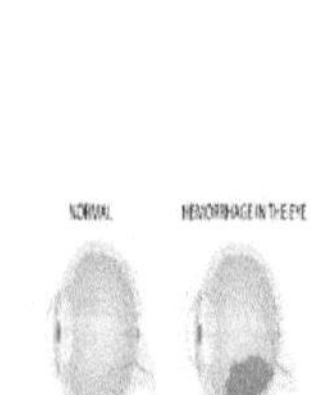

Wounded part→ especially cold to touch. (Not cold subjectively)

Some affection→ warmth of bed intolerable.

Due to→ heat & burning of limbs.

Physical generals→

Emaciation→ affected parts.

Pains→ sticking, tearing, throbbing. (Sensation)

Rheumatic pain. (< at night, warmth of bed and bed covering)

Ameliorated by→ holding feet in ice-water.

Eyes→ Hemorrhage:

Into→ anterior chamber. (After→ iridectomy)

Confusions of→ eyes & lids.

Especially→ if much extravasation of blood.

Ecchymosis→ of lids & conjunctiva.

Face→ Red pimples or tubercles.

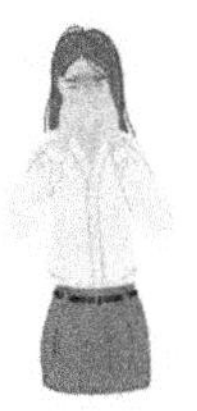

Site→ on forehead and cheeks.

As in brandy drinkers.

Stinging→ when touched.

Injuries→

Punctured wounds. (By→ sharp, pointed instruments)

Ex. As awls, nails, rat bites, stings of insects, esp.→ mosquito.

After injury→ long-remaining discoloration.

Black & blue places become green.

Extremities→ **(imp.)**

Rheumatism/ gout: Begin→ in lower limb. (Ascends)

By abuse of colchicum. (Low asthenic condition)

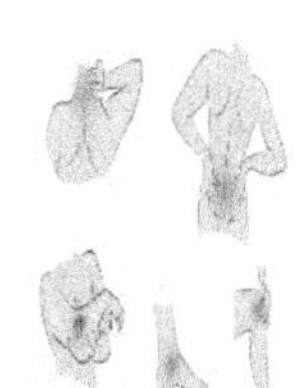

Painful→ Nodosites & gout stones→ joints. (Site)

Acute & chronic arthritis.

Affects→ left shoulder & Rt. Hip joint.

Swelling→ feet upto knees, knees, ball of great toe.

Unbearable pain→ during walking. (As from→ sprain/ false step)

In heels→ as if bruised.

Easy spraining→ ankles & feet.

Intense itching. (Site→ feet & ankles) < from scratching, warmth of bed.

LYCOPODIUM CLAVATUM

Common name→ Wolf's foot, club moss.

Family→ Lycopodiaceae.

Constitution→

Persons→ intellectually keen but physically weak.

Upper part of body→ emaciated.

Lower part→ semi-dropsical.

Lung & hepatic affections.

Especially→ extremes of life. (children & old people)

Children: weak, emaciated.

Well developed head.

Puny, sickly→ body.

Mental generals→ Ailments:

From fright, anger, mortification,

Vexation + reserved displeasure.

Avaricious, greedy, miserly, malicious, pusillanimous.

Irritable, cross (on walking), peevish.

Ugly, kick and scream, easily angered.

Can't endure opposition/ contradiction.

Seeks dispute→ beside himself.

Physical generals→

Deep-seated, progressive, chronic diseases.

Pains: Affection site→ Rt.-sided. (Chiefly)

Pain goes from right→ to left. (Throat, chest, abdomen, liver, ovaries)

Sensation→ aching-pressure, drawing.

<4-8p.m. (imp.)

Canine hunger→ more he eats, more he craves.

Headaches→ if he does not eat.

Waking at night→ feeling hungry.

Baby cries all day, sleeps all night.

General modalities→ Agg.→from 4-8 p.m. (All diseases)

Amel.→ warm food & drinks, uncovering head.

Loosening the garments.

Nose→ Catarrh:

Dry nose→ stopped at night. (Breath through mouth), snuffles.

Child start rubbing nose (from sleep) → root of nose,

Frontal sinuses, crusts, elastic plugs.

Face→ pale complexion.

Dirty, unhealthy, sallow + deep furrows.

Look old than his age.

Fan-like motion of alae nasi.(imp)

Throat→ Diphtheria:

Fauces→ brownish-red.

Deposit spread→ Rt. To left tonsil.

Descends→ nose to Rt. Tonsil.

< after sleep, from cold drinks.

Pneumonia: (neglected/ maltreated)

Site→ base of right lung. (To hasten absorption/ expectoration)

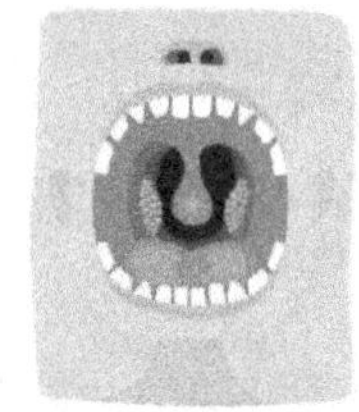

Urinary system→**(imp.)** Red sand in urine.

On→ child's diaper.

Child cries→ before urinating.

Associated symptom→ pain in back.

Relieved by→ urinating.

Renal colic. (Rt. sided)

Male rep. System→ Impotence: Of young men.

From→ sexual excess or onanism.

Penis→ small, cold, relaxed.

Old men with strong desire but imperfect erections.

During embrace fall asleep.

Premature emission.

Female rep. System→ Dryness of vagina.

Burning in→ during & after coition.

Foetus appears→ turning somersaults.

G.I.System→ (imp.)

Everything tastes→ sour. (Eructations, heart burn, waterbrash)

Sour vomiting. (Between chill and heat)

Constipation:

Since→ puberty, last confinement, when away from home.

Infant's constipation + ineffectual urging.

During stool→ rectum contracts & protrudes, discharge of blood from genitals.

Developing→ piles.

Hernia→ right sided. (Especially in children)

Gastric affection: Excessive accumulation of flatulence.

Constant→ satiety, good appetite.

Few mouthfuls fill up to the throat.

Feels→ bloated, fermentation in abdomen.

Associated symptoms→ loud grumbling, croaking. (Lower abdomen)

Fullness. (Belching gives no relief)

Respiratory system→ Pneumonia: (neglected/ maltreated)

Site→ base of right lung. (To hasten absorption/ expectoration)

Cough→ deep, hollow.

Little relief→ by raising mucus in large quantities.

Extremities→ One foot→ hot & Other one→ cold.

MAGNESIUM PHOSPHORICUM

Common name→ Magnesium phosphate or homoeopathic aspirin.

Chemical formula→ Mg3(PO4)2

Constitution→ Thin, emaciated person.

Highly nervous organization.

Dark complexion.

Physical generals→

Rt. Sided affection. (Head, ear, face, chest, ovary, sciatic nerve)

Pains: Unbearable

Sensation→ sharp, cutting, stabbing, constricting.

Shooting, stitching, lightning (like coming & going)

Intermittent peroxysm.

Pain→ driving patient to frenzy. (Changing place rapidly)

Cramping→ in neuralgic affection of→ stomach, abdomen, pelvis.

Great dread→ cold air, uncovering, touching affected part,

Cold bathing or washing, moving.

Languid, tired, exhausted.

Unable to→ sit up.

Ailments→ from standing in cold water/ working in cold clay.

General modalities→ **Agg.**→ Cold air, draft of cold air/ wind,

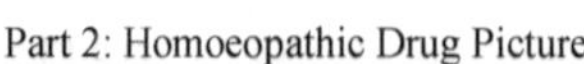

Cold bathing or washing, motion, touch.

Amel.→ Bending double, heat, warmth, pressure.

Particulars→

Head→ Headache: of school girl.

Begin→ in occiput.

Extend→ over head.

Face→ red & flushed.

Causation→ from mental exertion or hard study.

<10-11a.m. or 4-5p.m.

Ameliorated by→ pressure & external heat.

Face→ Neuralgia: intermittent.

Site→ face, supra or infra-orbital. (Rt.side)

Sensation→ darting, cutting.

< by touch, cold air, pressure.

Ameliorated by→ external heat.

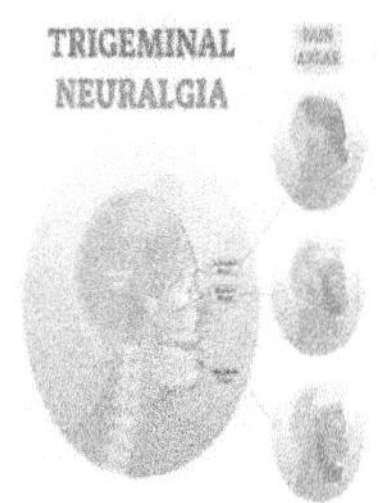

Mouth→

Ailments of teething children.

Spasm→ during dentition. (No fever)

Toothache→ at night. (Shifting rapidly)

< eating, drinking, especially cold things.

Ameliorated by→ heat.

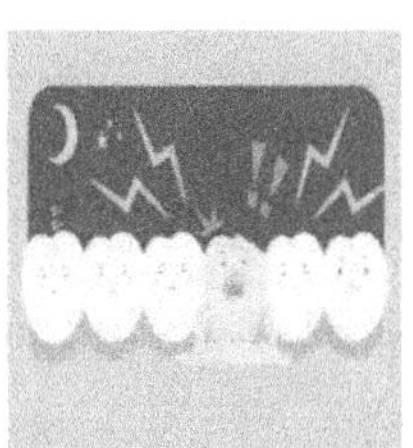

G.I.System→

Spasm & cramp of stomach.

Sensation→ as if tight band was drawn tightly around the body.

Tongue→ clean.

Colic→ flatulent, forcing to bend double.

Ameliorated by→ heat, rubbing and hard pressure.

Urinary system→ Nocturnal enuresis: after catheterization.

From→ nervous irritation.

Urine→ pale, copious.

Female rep. System→ Menses: Early.

Flow→ dark, stringy.

Pains:

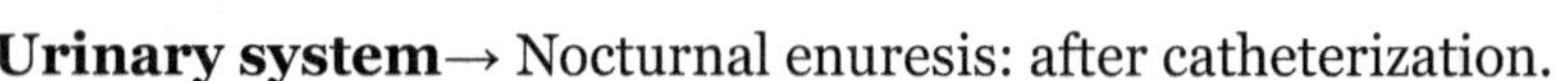

Sensation→ darting, like lightning, shooting.

Aggravation→ before menses, right side.

Amelioration→ when flow begins, by heat & bending double.

Vaginismus.

Nervous system→ Cramps:

Site→ extremities. (During pregnancy)

Of writers, piano or violin players.

NATRIUM MURIATICUM

Common name→ Common salt.

Chemical formula→ NaCl

Constitution→ Anemic & cathectic persons.

Cause→ from loss of vital fluids. (Profuse menses, seminal losses)

Mental affections.

Mental generals→ Ailments:

For bad effects of→ anger, grief, fright,

Vexation, mortification or reserved displeasure.

Irritable, awakward, hasty.

Drops things→ due to nervous weakness.

Child: cross→ when spoken to.

Crying→ from slightest cause.

Passion about trifles. (Especially→ during consolation)

Weeping disposition. (Marked)

Weeping mood→ without cause.

Consolation aggravates her trouble/complaints.

Dreams: robber in house.

Walking will not believe. (Until search is made)

Thirst→ burning.

Physical generals→

Great emaciated. (Children→ throat, neck→ emaciated during summer)

Loosing flesh→ while living well.

Great liability→ to take cold.

Craving→ for salt.

Aversion→ to bread.

Ailments→ bad effect of acid food,

Bread, quinine, excessive use of salts.

Cauterization of all kind + silver nitrate.

General modalities→ Agg.→ at 10 or 11 a.m., at seashore/sea air,

Heat of sun/ stove, mental exertion,

Talking, writing, reading, lying down.

Amel.→ in open air, cold bathing, lying on rt. Side.

Going without regular meal.

Particulars→

Head→ Headache: (School girls)

Anemic.

From→ sunrise to sunset.

Site→ let-sided clavus.

Beginning→ with blindness & zig-zag dazzling. (Lightning in eyes)

Sensation→ bursting, red face, nausea & vomiting,

During & after→ menses.

As though thousand little hammer knocking in brain. (During→ fever)

Throbbing headache from→ eye strain.

When touched→ Hair falls out sensation. (In nursing women)

Face→ oily, shiny, greased.

Ameliorated by→ perspiration.

Eyes→ Lachrymation.

Tears→ stream down during coughing.

Mouth→

Sensation as→ hair on the tongue.

Tongue: mapped, with red insular patches,

Like→ ringworm on sides.

Heavy, difficult speech, children slow in learning to walk.

G.I.System→

Constipation:

Sensation of→ contraction of anus; torn, bleeding,

Smarting→ afterwards

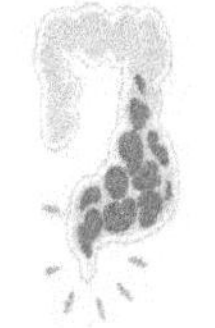

Stool→ dry, hard, difficult, crumbling.

Involuntary stool→ knows not whether flatus or faeces escape .

Stitches→ in rectum.

Urinary system→ Urine:

Involuntary→ during walking, coughing, laughing.

Cutting in→ urethra. (After passage of urine)

Has to wait a long while or urine to pass. (if others are present)

Male rep. System→ Seminal emission: (Soon after→ coition)

Increased desire.

Weakness→ of sexual organs + retarted emission during an embrace.

After sexual excesses→ impotence, spinal irritation, paralysis.

Female rep. System→

Sensation→ Pressing, pushing. (Towards genitals every morning)

Must sit down→ to prevent prolapsus.

Respiratory system→ Hay fever:

Sensation→ squirming sensation in the nostril, as of a small worm.

Cause→ by exposure to hot sun or intense summer heat.

Cardio-vascular system→

Fluttering of heart.

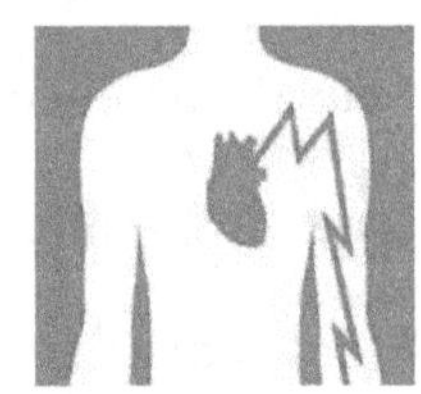

Sensation→ weak, faint feeling.

< lying down.

Heart's pulsations shake the body.

Extremities→

Painful contractions of→ hamstrings.

Fever→

Fever blisters. (like pearls about the lips)

Lips→ dry, sore, cracked& ulcerated.

Intermittents: (Paroxysm at 10 or 11 a. m.)

Old, chronic, badly treated case.

Especially→ after suppression by quinine.

Headache + unconsciousness (During chill and heat)

Sweat > pains.

Skin→

Hangnails: skin around the nails dry and cracked.

Herpes about anus and on borders of hair at nape of neck.

Warts→ on palms of hand.

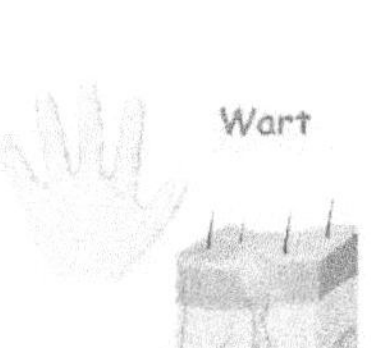

Eczema; raw, red, inflamed.

Especially→ in edges of hair.

< from eating too much salt, at sea shore, or from ocean voyage.

Urticaria. (Acute or chronic)

Over whole body, especially after violent exercise.

NATRUM PHOSPHORICUM

Common name→ Phosphate of soda / Sodium phosphate.

Chemical formula→Na_2HPO_4

Mental generals→

Imagines, on waking at night,

pieces of furniture are persons.

Hears→ footsteps in next room. Fear.

Particulars→

Head→

Sensation→ Dull in morning,

full feeling & throbbing.

Eyes→

Discharge→ golden-yellow, creamy matter.

Dilation of one pupil & Whites of eyes dirty yellow.

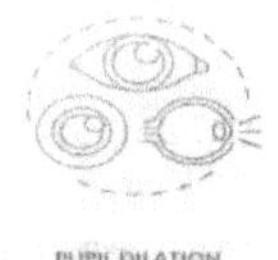

Ears→ One ear red, hot & frequently itchy.

Concomitant→ gastric derangements & acidity.

Respiratory system→

Itching of nose.

Naso-pharyngeal catarrh.

Mucus→ thick, yellow & offensive. (Odour→ offensive)

Face→

Paleness of bluish & appearance→ florid.

Mouth→ Canker sores of lip &cheeks.

Tongue→ Thin, moist coating on tongue.

Blisters on tip with stinging in evening.

Yellow, creamy coating at back part of roof of the mouth.

Dysphagia.

G.I.System→ Sour eructations & vomiting.

Diarrhoea→ greenish.

Spits mouthful of food.

Male→ Gonorrhoea.

Emissions without dreams.

Concomitant weakness in back and trembling in limbs. Desire without erection. Gonorrhoea.

Female→

Menses→ Pale, thin, watery. (Too early)

Sterility with acid secretions from vagina.

Leucorrhoea. (Discharge creamy / honey-colored or acid & watery)

Associated symptoms→ Morning sickness + sour vomiting.

Extremities→

Rheumatism of the knee-joint.

Hamstring sore.

Rheumatoid arthritis.

Skin→ Yellow.

Itching especially of ankles.

Hives. (Appearance→ Smooth, red, shining)

Erysipelas. (Feet icy cold in daytime, burn at night)

Swelling of lymphatic glands.

NATRUM SULPHURICUM

Common name→ Sodium sulphate.

Chemical formula→ $NaOSO_3. 10Aq$

Constitution→

Patient feels→ every change from dry to wet.

Can't tolerate sea air.

Can't eat plants that thrive near water.

Constitution in which→ gonorrhoeal poison is most pernicious.

Slowly recovering. (From every sickness)

Skin affections reappear→ every spring. (imp.)

Mental generals→ Mental traumatism:

Injuries to head. (Mental effect)

Chronic brain effects of blows, falls.

Inability to think.

Irritable, sad, gloomy. (worse in mornings)

Dislikes to speak / be spoken to.

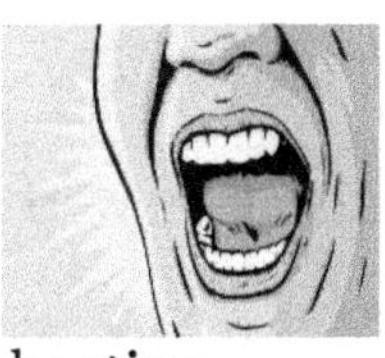

Depressed; lively music→ makes her sad.

Satiety of like; must use great self-control to prevent shooting himself.

General modalities→ **Agg.**→ Damp basements / dwellings,

damp weather, lying, rest.

Amel.→ Dry weather, pressure, sitting up (cough), changing position, open air.

Must change position frequently. (painful & gives little relief)

Physical generals→ Ailments:

Aggravated by→ dampness of weather, damp houses / cellars.

Eyes→ Granular lids:

Like→ small blisters.

Green pus + terrible photophobia. (gonorrhoeal / sycotic)

Nose→

Nose bleed→ during menses.

Mouth→ Toothache:

> by cold water, cool air.

Tongue→ Dirty, greenish-gray or brown coating.

G.I.System→ (imp.)

Diarrhoea: (First rising and standing on feet)

Sudden, urging, gushing, much flatus.

Cause: After→ spell of wet weather.

Living on working in basements.

Make rep. System→ Gonorrhoea:

Discharge→ Greenish-yellow, painless, thick,

Chronic/ suppressed.

Respiratory system→ (imp.) Dyspnoea:

Desire→ to take a deep breath. (during damp, cloudy weather)

Humid asthma→ in children.

Cause→ every change to wet weather& every fresh cold.

Worse→ in damp, rainy weather.

Sputa→ green, greenish, copious.

Sycotic pneumonia: site→ lower lobe of left lung.

Associated symp.→ great soreness of chest, during cough,

Sit up in bed and hold the chest with both hands.

Nervous system→ Spinal meningitis:

Sensation→ Violent crushing gnawing pains at base of brain.

Head drawn back.

Spasms + mental irritability &delirium.

Associated symp.→ violent congestion of blood to head,

delirium; opisthotonos.

Nux vomica

Common name→ Poison Nut

Family→ Loganiaceae.

Constitution→ Best remedies→ to commence treatment of cases:

Drugged by mixtures, bitters, vegetable pills,

Nostrums or quack remedies, especially aromatic or "hot medicines."

Adapted→ to thin, irritable, careful, zealous persons.

Dark hair &temperament→ bilious or sanguine.

Disposed→ to be quarrelsome, spiteful, malacious,

Nervous &melancholic.

Debauchers→ thin, irritable, nervous disposition.

Prone to indigestion & haemorrhoids.

Anxiety + irritability & inclination to suicide. (But afraid to die)

"Nux is chiefly successful with persons of an ardent character; of an irritable, impatient temperament, disposed to anger, spite or deception." – Hahnemann.

Hypochondriac: literary, studious persons.

Who are→ too much at home. (want of exercise)

Complaints→ gastric, abdominal complaints and costiveness.

Especially→ in drunkards.

Mental generals→

Persons→ very particular, careful.

Inclined to→ easily excited or angered,

irascible & tenacious.

Physical generals→ Ailments:

Bad effects of→ coffee, tabacco, alcoholic stimulants,

Highly spiced / seasoned food & over-eating.

Long continued mental over- exertion.

Sedentary habits.

Loss of sleep.

Aromatic or patent medicines.

Sitting on cold stones. (especially→ in warm weather)

Oversensitive to→ external impressions, noise, odors,

light or music.

Trifling ailments→ unbearable.

Every harmless word offends.

Pains: Sensation→ tingling, sticking, hard, aching.

< from motion and contact.

Tendency to faint,

From→ odors; in morning; after eating; after every labor pain.

Falling asleep→ in evening, reading hours. (Before bad time)

Wakes→ at 3 or 4 a. m.

Dreamy sleep at daybreak. (Hard to arouse)

Depression of spirits→ after eating.

Feels tired and weak.

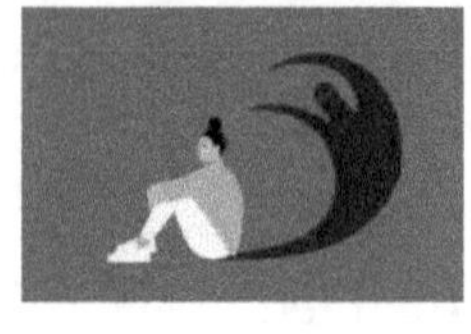

General modalities→ Agg.→Morning: waking at 4 a. m.,

mental exertion, after→ eating / over-eating.

Touch, noise, anger, spices, narcotics, dry weather & cold air.

Amel.→ In evening, during rest,

Lying down, and in damp, wet weather.

Particulars→

Nose→ Catarrh:

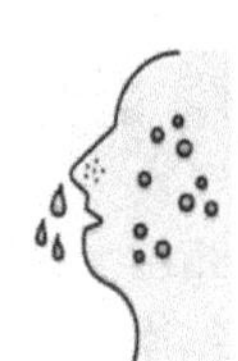

Snuffles of infants.

Coryza→ dry at night, fluent by day.

<in warm room.

> in cold air; sitting→ in cold places, on stone steps.

G.I.System→(imp.)

Eructations→ sour & bitter; GERD.

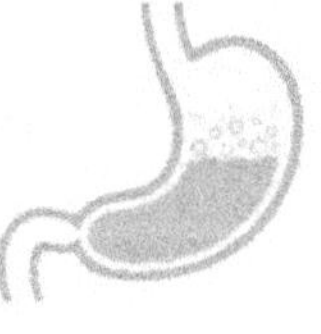

Nausea & vomiting→ every morning. (Constant)

Causation→ after eating, from smoking.

Sensation→ "If I could only vomit I would be so much better."

Stomach: pressure 1-2 hr. after eating as from stone.

Can't use the mind & sleepy for 2-3 hours after a meal.

Pyrosis, tightness, loosen clothing.

Strangulated hernia. (Especially→ umbilical)

Alternate constipation & diarrhoea.

Persons→ take purgatives for long time.

Constipation→ Unsuccessful desire + small quantity of feces.

From→ anxiety, worry, brandy, coffee,

drugs, night watching, high living, etc.

Sensation→ as not finished, frequent desire for stool;

Anxious & ineffectual.

Amel.→ for a time after stool; in morning after rising;

after mental exertion.

Female rep. System→

Menses→ too early, profuse, too long lasting,

every two weeks, irregular, never at right time,

stopping & starting again.

Complaints→ at onset & remaining after menses.

During &after menses< of old symptoms.

Labor pains→ violent & spasmodic.

Pain cause→ urging to stool / urinate.

< in back; prefers a warm room.

Back→

Backache: (Must→ sit up to turn over in bed)

Lumbago. (Causation→ from sexual weakness & masturbation)

Nervous system→ (imp.)

Convulsions with consciousness.

Agg.→ anger, emotion, touch, moving.

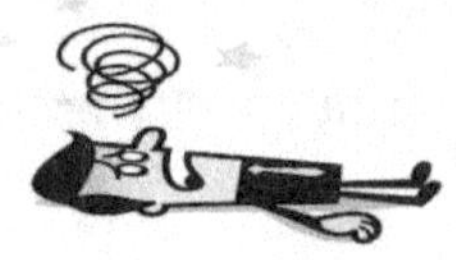

Fever→

Chilly→ on least movement; from being uncovered,

Must→ covered in every stage of fever – chill, heat or sweat.

Repugnance to cold or cold air.

Fever: great heat, whole body burning hot.

Face→ red & hot.

Patient can't move or uncover without being chilly.

PULSATILLA NIGRICANS

Common name→ Anemone.

Family→ Ranunculaceae.

Constitution→

Adapted to→ indecisive, slow,

phelgmatic persons (temperament)

Appearance→ Sandy hair, blue eyes, pale face.

Easily moved to laughter / tears.

Affectionate, mild, gentle, timid, yielding disposition .

"The woman's remedy".

Women inclined to be fleshy,

Menstruation→ scanty & protracted.

Mental generals→

Weeps easily:

Impossible to detail her ailments without weeping.

Feels better by consolation. (Ameliorate)

Physical generals→

Especially in→ diseases of women & children.

1st serious impairment of health is referred to puberic age.

Have "never been well since".

Ex. anaemia, chlorosis, bronchitis, phthisis.

Secretions→ thick, bland and yellowish- green.

From→ all mucus membrane.

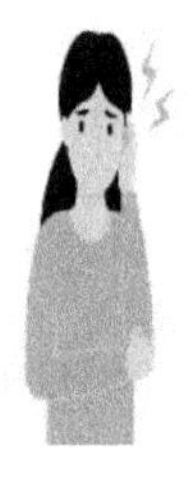

No two chills, no two stools, no two attacks alike.

Symptoms→ ever changing; apparently contradictory.

Very well one hour, very miserable the next.

Pains→ Rapidly shifting from one part to another, on first motion.

Sensation→ drawing, tearing, erratic.

Associated symptoms→ constant chilliness; more severe pain, more sever chill.

Appear suddenly & leave gradually.

General modalities→ Agg.→ In warm close room; evening,

at twilight; on first move; very rich, fat, indigestible food.

Lying on left, or on painless side, warm applications, heat.

Pressure on well side if it be made toward the diseased side.

Amel.→ In open air; lying on painful side, cold applications.

Cold air or cool room, eating or drinking cold things.

Particulars→

Eyes→ Styes:

Especially→ on upper lid.

Causation→ from eating fat, greasy, rich food or pork .

Mouth→

Great dryness of mouth. (In the morning)

Thirst→ absent.

Toothache: Ameliorate→ by holding cold water in the mouth.

Aggravate→ from warm things and heat of room.

G.I.System→

Gastric difficulties.

Causation→ from eating rich food, cake, pastry.

Especially after pork or sausage.

The sight or even the thought of port causes disgust.

"bad taste" in the morning.

"All-gone" sensation in stomach. (Esp.→ in tea drinkers)

Diarrhoea: usually at night.

Stool→ watery, greenish-yellow,

Very changeable soon as they eat.

Causation→ from fruit, cold food or drinks, ice-cream.

Female rep. System→

Derangements at puberty.

Menses→ too late, scanty, slimy, painful, irregular.

Intermitting flow. (More→ during day)

Suppressed→ from getting feet wet.

Concomitant→ evening chilliness, intense pain,

great restlessness and tossing about.

Delayed→ first menstruation.

Threatened abortion.

Flow→ ceases& then returns with increased force.

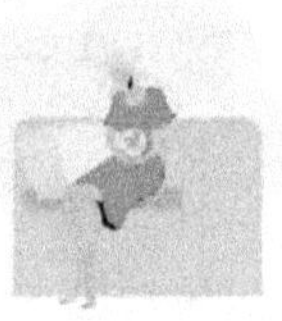

Pains→ spasmodic, excite suffocation and fainting. (Crave→ fresh air)

Respiratory system→

Unable to breathe well & chilly in warm room.

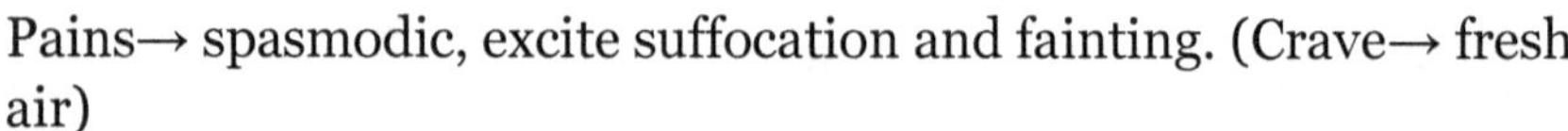

Extremities→

Nervousness. (Intensely→ felt about the ankles)

RHUS TOXICODENDRON

Common name→ Poison Oak.

Family→ Anacardiaceae.

Constitution→

Adapted to→ rheumatic diathesis persons.

Mental generals→

Great apprehension at night.

Fears→ he will die of being poisoned.

Can't remain in bed.

Dreams→ of great exertion, rowing, swimming,

working hard at his / her daily occupation.

Physical generals→ Ailments: Bad effects of getting wet,

Especially→ after being overheated.

From→ spraining or straining a single part,

muscle or tendon, overlifting,

Particularly→ from stretching high up to reach things,

Lying on damp ground,

Too much summer bathing in lake or river.

Affects→ fibrous tissue. (Especially→ right side more)

Pains: as if→ sprained,

A muscle or tendon was torn from its attachment,

Bones were scrapped with knife.

Particular agg.→ after midnight and in wet, rainy weather.

Affected parts sore to touch.

Great restlessness, anxiety, apprehension.

Must change position often to obtain relief.

Restless, can't stay long in one position.

Great sensitiveness to open air.

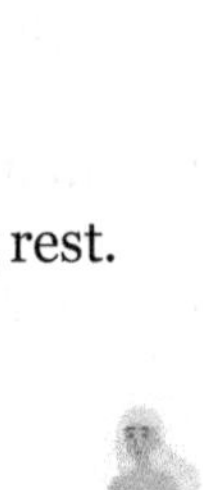

Putting hand from underbed - cover brings on cough.

Dry→ tongue, mouth & throat. (Thirst→ great)

General modalities→ **Agg.**→ Before storm, during rest.

Cold, wet & rainy weather.

At night. (Especially→ after midnight)

from getting wet→ perspiring.

Amel.→ Warm, dry→ weather.

Wrapping up→ warm / hot things.

Motion, changing position.(moving→ affected parts)

The great characteristic of Rhus.→

Pain: < during repose and are > by motion. (Few exception)

Particulars→

Head→ Vertigo,

During→ standing / walking.

worse when lying down

Particular modality→ < when lying down,

<rising from lying, stooping.

Headache:

Sensation→ Brain loosing (when stepping / shaking head) ,

And swashing in brain, stupefying, as if torn→ from beer,

Returns→ from least chagrin.

< from sitting, lying, in cold,

> warmth & motion.

Face→ Ulcers:

Site→ Corners of mouth.

Fever blisters.

Site→ around mouth & on chin.

Mouth→

Tongue: dry, sore, red, cracked. (Tip→ triangular red)

And takes imprint of

G.I.System→ Diarrhoea: (involuntary)

DRY MOUTH

With→ beginning typhoid & great exhaustion.

Sensation of pain→

Tearing down the posterior part of limbs during stool.

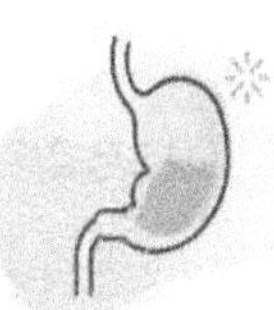

Male rep. System→

Inflammation, erisiplatous, oedematous.

Site→ External genitalia.

Respiratory system→

Cough + taste of blood.

Dry, teasing cough:

Occurrence→ before and during chill, in intermittent fever.

Back→

Pain & swallowing→ between the shoulders.

Pain & stiffness→ in small of back.

< sitting or lying, > by motion or lying on something hard.

Extremities→

Lameness, stiffness & pain.

Complaint→ on first moving (After rest)

on getting up in the morning.

> by walking or continued motion.

Muscular rheumatism, sciatica. (On left side)

Aching in left arm. (With→ heart disease)

Nervous system→

Paralysis, numbness of affected parts.

Causation→ from getting wet, lying on damp ground,

ague or typhoid, paresis of limbs, ptosis,

after exertion, parturition, sexual excesses.

Fever→

Occurrence→ When acute diseases assume a typhoid form.

Skin→

Erysipelas. (From→ left to right)

Vesicular. (Vesicles→ yellow)

Swelling & inflammation.

Sensation→ burning, itching, stinging.

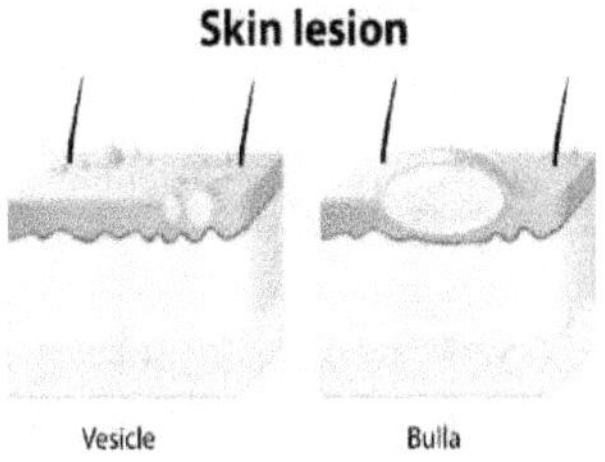

Skin lesion

Vesicle

Bulla

RUTA GRAVEOLENS

Common name→ Rue.

Family→ Rutaceae.

Physical generals→

All parts of body→ are painful. (Upon he lies)

Sensation→ as if bruised lame, restless(Esp.→ when lying)

as after a fall or blow.

Turns &changes position. (Frequently)

Worse in limbs and joints (Arn.).

Particulars→

Eyes→

Aching in & over eyes.

Associated symptoms→ blurred vision, eye strained.

Ailments→ After using eyes at fine work,

Ex. watchmaking, engraving & looking intently.

Amblyopia or asthenopia.

Ailments→ from over-exertion of eyes, over-use in bad light

Or refraction anomalies, fine sewing, over-reading at night.

Misty, dim vision.

Associated symptom→ complete obscuration at a distance.

Sensation→ Eyes burn, ache, strained;

hot, like balls of fire, lower lids spasm.

G.I.System→

Constipation,

Ailments→ from inactivity, or impaction.

Following→ mechanical injuries.

Prolapse of rectum,

Ailments→ immediately on attempting a passage,

from the slightest stooping; after confinement,

frequent unsuccessful urging.

Urinary system→

Pressure on bladder.

Sensation→ as if constantly full.

Continues after urinating.

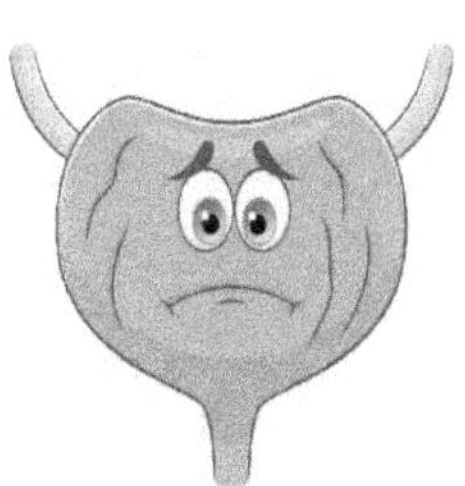

Hardly retain urine on account of urging.

Difficult voiding after urine retention.

Urine→ scanty green. (Frequency→ involuntary)

Respiratory system→ Phthisis,

After→ mechanical injuries to chest.

Back→ Backache,

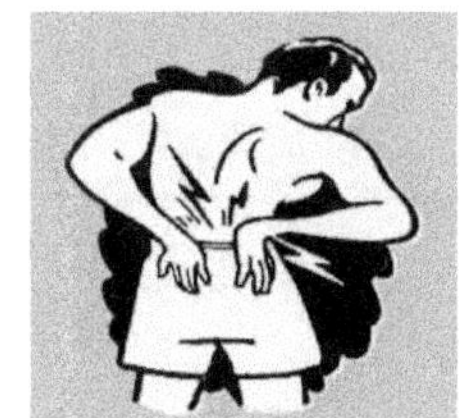

Ameliorate→ by lying on back.

Extremities→

Lameness after sprains. (Especially→ wrists & ankles)

Skin→

Warts; (Appearance→ flat& smooth)

Site→ on palms of hands

Sensation→ sore pains.

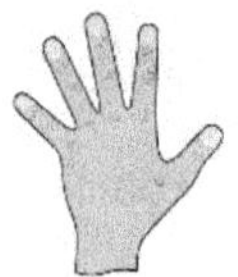

SILICEA TERA

Common name→ Pure Silica.

Chemical formula→ silicic oxide.

Constitution→ Silicea→ chronic of Pulsatilla.

Temperament→ Nervous, irritable, sanguine.

Diathesis→ Psoric.

Appearance→ light complexion, dry, skin;

Pale face, weakly + lax muscles + distended abdomen,

Slow in learning to walk. (cause→ ankle weak)

Constitutions→ suffer from deficient nutrition,

Cause→ imperfect assimilation.

Oversensitive→ physically & mentally.

Scrofulous, rachitic children.

Head→ large & open fontanelles.

Extreme→ perspiration about the head. (Kept warm the head)

distended abdomen; weak ankles; slow in learning to walk.

Mental generals→ Children:

Obstinate, headstrong, restless, fidgety,

Cry→ spoken kindly to.

Starts at least noise.

Anxious, yielding & fainthearted.

Mental labor extremely difficult.

Can't bear to think.

Fatigue→ from reading & writing.

Physical generals→ Ailments:

Bad effects of vaccination. (Esp.→ abscess & convulsions)

Suppressed foot-sweat.

exposing to slight draught of air. (Head or back)

chest complaints→ total loss of strength. (Stonecutters)

Great weariness & nervous debility.

Exhaustion with erythism.

Causation→ from hard work & close confinement.

Overcome→ by force of will.

Chilly→ Want of vital heat, even after taking active exercise.

Takes cold from exposure of feet.

Desire→ to be magnetized.

Maturing abscesses & reducing excessive suppuration.

Night walking; gets up→ walk→ lies down again.

Promotes→ expulsion of foreign bodies from tissues.

Ex. Bone splinters, fish bones, needles.

Inflammation, swelling &suppuration of glands.

Ex. cervical, axillary, inguinal, sebaceous,

Parotid, mammary etc. (malignant & gangrenous)

Sweat of hands, toes, feet and axillae; offensive.

General modalities→ Agg.→ Cold, during menses& new moon, uncovering(Esp.→ the head), lying down.

Amel.→ Warmth (Esp.→ wrapping up the head)

Exception→ gastric complaint. (> by cold food)

Particulars→

Head→Vertigo:

Origin→ spinal.

Ascending→ from back of neck to head.

Sensation→ as if one would fall forward. (From→ looking up)

Chronic sick headaches:

Past history→ since some severe disease of youth.

Ascending→ from nape of neck to the vertex.

Sensation→ as if coming from spine.

Locating→ in one eye. (Especially→ the right)

Particular modalities→

< draught of air or uncovering head.

> profuse urination.

> pressure & wrapping up warmly.

Eyes→

Fistula lachrymalis.

G.I.System→ Constipation:

Occurrence→ before and during menses.

Difficult stool: Sensation→ great straining,

As if rectum was paralyzed.

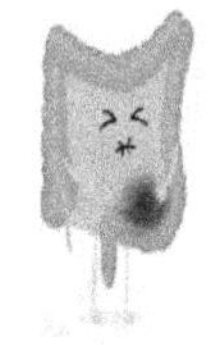

Causation→ as from inactivity of rectum.

Stool→ partly expelled & recedes again.

Fissura ani→ extreme pain. (After stool)

Faeces→ remain long time in rectum,

Alternate→ chest symptoms.

Female rep. System→

Discharge of blood.

Site→ from vagina.

Occurrence→ every time child takes breast.

Drawn nipple. (Like→ a funnel)

Extremities→ Intolerable pain.

Feet→ cold, sour & carrion-like odour. (Every evening)

Perspiration→ absent.

Skin→ Skin→ Unhealthy & little injury suppurates.

Crippled nails: site→ on fingers & toes.

Ingrowing→ toe-nails.

Panaritium, carbuncles; ulcers, blood boils.

Fistulae→ painful, fleshy, offensive, high spongy edges.

SPONGIA TOSTA

Common name→ Roasted sponge.

Family→ Spongia.

Constitution→

Tubercular diathesis.

Adapted to diseases of children & women. (Especially)

Appearance→ light hair, lax fiber & fair complexion.

Physical generals→

< after sleep.

Sweat. < after midnight.

Goitre, swelling & induration of glands.

Throat→

Complaint→ Sore throat.

Particular modalities→ < after eating sweet things.

Make rep. System→

Testicles→ swollen, bruised & squeezed.

Spermatic cord→ swollen & painful.

Causation→ after suppressed gonorrhoea or maltreated orchitis.

Respiratory system→ **(Imp.)** Suffocating:

Sensation→ as if head to breathe through a sponge.

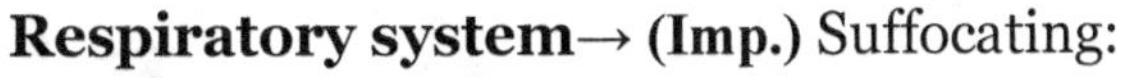

Throat, larynx, trachea, bronchi – "dry as a horn."

No mucous rale.

Cough <mental excitement

Cough: dry, barking & croupy,

rasping, ringing, wheezing & whistling.

Sibilant cough→ like a saw driven through a pine board.

<mental excitement, sweets, cold drinks,

smoking, lying with head low, dry cold winds.

< reading, singing, talking & swallowing.

> eating or drinking warm things.

Croup: anxious & wheezing.

< during inspiration& before midnight.

Cardiovascular system→ Palpitation: violent.

Associated symp.→ pain & gasping respiration.

Awakened suddenly after midnight.

Sensation→ suffocative & great anxiety.

Valvular insufficiency:

Occurrence→ before & during menses.

Angina pectoris: Sensation→ contracting pain, heat,

Faintness, suffocation & anxiety.

Neck→ Goitre. Thyroid gland swollen. (Also→ chin)

Suffocative paroxysyms. (At→ night)

SULPHUR

Common name→ Brimstone; Flowers of sulphur.

Chemical composition→ The element.

Constitution→

Diathesis→ scrofulous.

Subject to→ portal system congestion.

Lean, stoop-shouldered persons.

Walk & sit→ stooping like old men. (imp.)

Temperament→ nervous.

Quick tempered & plethoric person.

Skin extremely sensitive to atmospheric changes.

Children: Have→ worms.

Emaciated & big-bellied.

Can't bear bathing or washing.

Restless, hot, kick off the clothes. (At→ night)

Dirty, filthy people. (Prone→ to skin affections)

Mental generals→

Too unhappy to live & lazy to rouse.

Happy dreams + wakes up singing.

Everything looks pretty. (Rags also→ seem beautiful)

Movement in abdomen. (Sensation→ as of a child)

Physical generals→

Aversion→ bathing & washing.

Increase the reactive power of human system.

Relapsing complaints→ Ex. menses, leucorrhoea etc.

Disease returns again & again.

Congestion& malignant of growth of any organ,

Occurrence→ esp. at climacteric.

Sensation: burning→ on vertex,

smarting→ eyes & face (Redness absent)

Mouth vesicles& dryness of throat. (Rt.→ left)

Dryness in→ stomach, rectum, anus & itching piles.

Hot flushes. (During→ day)

Passing→ weak, faint spells + little moisture.

Urine→ scalding, large quantities& colorless.

Sensation→ like fire in ripples.

Site→ chest, rising to face, skin.

Psoric, chronic diseases.

Causation→ from suppressed eruptions.

Standing→ worst position for Sulphur pt.

Every standing position→ uncomfortable.

Dropsy & chronic alcoholism.

Discharge→ acrid, excoriating.

Ex. urine & faeces.

Painful→ to parts over which it passes.

All orifice→ extreme red & excoriated.

Facilitate absorption of serous or inflammatory exudates.

Site→ in brain, pleura, lungs, joints.

General modalities→

Agg.→At rest & standing; warmth in bed,

Changing of weather, washing & bathing.

Amel.→ Lying on right side, dry & warm weather.

Particulars→

Head→

Sick headache.

Occurrence→ every 1-2 weeks.

Concomitant→ prostrating, weakening.

Constant hot vertex & cold feet.

Mouth→

Blood would burst through lip. (Bright red)

G.I.System→

Empty & faint feeling in the stomach. (Time→ 11 a. m.)

Weak, faint spells.

Occurrence→ during the day.

Diarrhoea: painless

Occurrence→ after midnight.

Compel→ driving out of bed in early morning.

Sensation→ as if bowels were too weak to retain its contents.

Constipation:

Constipation alternate with diarrhoea.

Stools→ large, dry, hard, knotty. (Painful)

Child→ pain compels child to desist on first effort.

Haemorrhoids. (Past treated→ with ointments)

Female rep. System→ Menorrhagia:

Has not been well, (since→ her last miscarriage)

Menses: too early, profuse & protracted.

"A single dose at new moon." – Lippe.

Respiratory system→

Suffocative attacks, suddenly wide awake. (At→ night)

Desire→ doors and windows open.

Drowsy: Occurrence→ in afternoon after sunset.

Wakefulness whole night.

Extremities→

Cold feet. (At→ daytime)

Burning soles. (At→ night)

Cramps in calves & soles. (At→ night)

Find a cool place for feet.

Puts feet out of bed to cool off.

Skin→ Boils:

Occurrence→ in crops,

Single boil is succeeded by another. (After→ first healed)

Site→ various parts of the body.

Skin: burning, voluptuous, itching & scratching.

Particular modalities→ < from soreness in folds, heat of bed.

>"feels good to scratch"

Skin affections→ treated by medicated soaps & washes.

SYMPHYTUM OFFICINALE

Common name→ Comfrey.

Family→ Borraginaceae.

Particulars→

Eyes→

Sensation→ Pain in eye.

Causation→ after a blow of an obtuse body,

snow ball strikes the eye,

Infant thrusts fist into its mother's eyes.

Injuries→

For→ fracture & mechanical injuries. (Excellent remedy)

Facilitates union of fractured bone.

Lessens peculiar pricking pain.

Favours→ production of callous. (Nervous origin trouble)

Sensation→

Irritability. (Site→ at point of fracture)

Periosteal pain. (After wounds have healed)

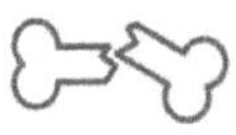

FRACTURE

Mechanical injuries:

Blows, bruises, thrusts on the globe of the eye.

THUJA OCCIDENTALIS

Common name→ Tree of life, White Cedar.

Family→ Coniferae.

Constitution→

Hydrogenoid constitution of Grauvogl.

Thuja related to the sycosis of Hahnemann –

fig warts, condylomata & wart-like excrescences.

Site→ upon mucous surfaces.

Lymphatic temperament, very fleshy persons,

dark complexion, black hair & unhealthy skin.

Mental generals→

Fixed ideas→

As strange person were his side,

soul and body were separated,

a living animal were in abdomen.

Under the influence of superior power.

Insane women will not be approached.

Physical generals→

Ailments→ from bad effects of vaccination,

suppressed or maltreated gonorrhoea.

Sensation→ as if body made of glass & break easily. (Esp.→ limbs)

as if beaten, from→ bone.

Chill. (Beginning→ in thighs)

Sweat: on uncovered parts, all over except the head.

Profuse, sour smelling & fetid at night.

Starts→ when he sleeps.

Stops→ when he wakes.

Perspiration→ smelling like honey. (Site→ on genitals)

General modalities→ Agg.→At 3 a.m. & 3 p.m.

At night, from heat of bed, from cold damp air& narcotics.

Particulars→

Head→ Vertigo:

Occurrence→ when closing the eyes.

Headache:

Origin→ Chronic, sycotic or syphilitic.

Sensation→ as if a nail driven into parietal bone.

as if a convex button were pressed on the part.

< from sexual excesses, overheating from tea.

White scaly dandruff. Hair dry & falling out.

Eyes→

Ophthalmia neonatorum.

Large granulations. (Like→ warts or blisters)

Origin→ Sycotic or syphilitic.

> by warmth & covering.

Eyelids: Agglutinated at night.

Dry, scaly. (Site→ on edges)

Styes & tarsal tumors.

Chalazae: thick, hard knots. (Like→ small condylomata)

Ears→

Chronic otitis:

Discharge→ purulent. (Like→ putrid meat)

Polypi: pale red, cellular. (Bleeding→ easily)

Granulations, condylomata.

Nose→ Chronic catarrh:

Occurrence→ after exanthemata.

Mucus→ thick & green. (With blood & pus)

Mouth→

Teeth decay & crumble.

Site→ at the roots. (Crowns remain sound)

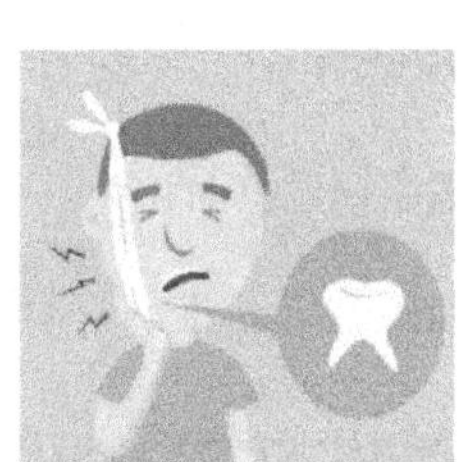

Turn→ yellow.

Toothache: from→ tea drinking.

Ranula: bluish in colour.

Varicose veins→ on tongue or in mouth.

G.I.System→ Abdomen:

Sensation→ motion as if something alive & animal crying,

Protrudes here and there like arm of a foetus

Constipation:

Sensation→ Violent pains in rectum.

Compel→ cessation of effort.

Stool→ recedes, after being partly expelled.

Piles: swollen,

Pain→ severe when sitting.

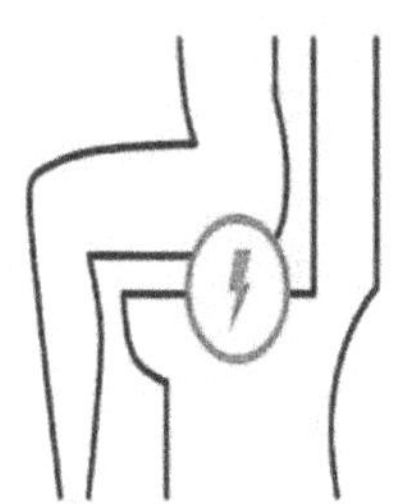

Diarrhoea:

Occurrence→ early morning.

Stool→ expelled forcibly + much flatus.

Gurgling sound→ as water from a bunghole.

< after breakfast, onions, coffee, fat food, vaccinations.

Anus: fissured & painful to touch.

Surrounded→ with flat warts Or moist mucous condylomata.

Urinary system→

Sensation→ as of urine trickling in urethra. (After urination)

Severe cutting:

Site→ at close of urination.

Male rep. System→

Articular rheumatism, prostatitis & sycosis.

Impotence; condylomata & many constitutional troubles.

Causation→ suppressed gonorrhoea

Female rep. System→

Sensation→ Distressing & burning pain.

Site→ in left ovarian region.

Occurrence→ when walking or riding.

Compel→ sit or lie down.

<at each menstrual nisus.

Extreme sensitiveness of vagina,

Thus→ coition prevented.

Extremities→

Limbs feel as if made of wood. (During→ walking)

Skin→

Dirty& brownish-white spots here and there.

Warts→ large, seedy & pedunculated.

Eruptions→ only on covered parts.

Sensation→ burn after scratching.

Nails: deformed& brittle.

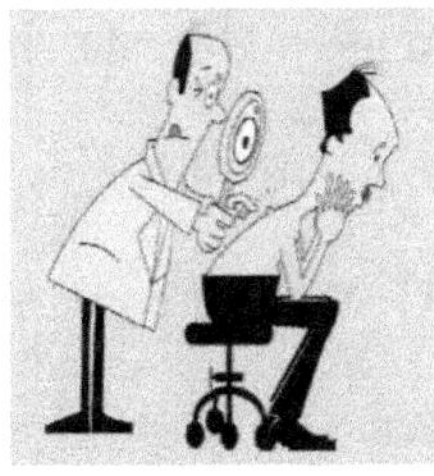

Appendix I

BHMS-II Materia Medica

Imp. university examination questions

Q. What is symptom?

Ans. The word symptom has been derived from the word `symptoma' which means ` anything that happens'.

 A symptom can be defined as an external expression of the internally deranged vital force.

According to Doctor Hahnemann "the change in the health of the body and of the mind which can be perceived externally by means of senses, that is to say, he notice only the deviations from the former healthy state to the now diseased individual, which are felt by the patient himself, remarked by the those around him and observed by the physician.

Eg. Any medicine 1 or 2 symptoms.

Q. Write about Ailments from/causation?

Ans. Definition-"Cause of the disease or illness, which can be present at the mental level as well as physical level to produce disease."

Eg. Any 2,3 medicines ailments from.

Q. Sphere of action or mode of action?

Ans. Symptomatology of the medicine emphasizing the characteristic symptoms. (mental, physical generals and particulars including sensations, modalities. And concomitants) and constitution.

It commonly involves the major site or part of the individual person during the period of remedial action.

Eg. Any 2,3 medicines sphere of action.

Q. What is complete symptom or Grand symptom or Qualified symptom?

Ans. According to Dr. Boenninghausen the doctrine of complete symptom, each 'grand' or complete symptom should consist of the following components: 1) Location, 2) Sensation, 3) Modalities, 4) Concomitant.

Eg. Any 1,2 medicines 1 or 2 complete symptoms.

Q. Write about modalities?

Ans. Definition-Modality is the circumstances and condition that affect or modify a symptom.

AGGRAVATION-Aggravation means increase the condition due to any circumstances. It is denoted as using symbol "<" or abbreviation "agg"

AMELIORATION-Amelioration which gives relief or reduce the intensity of symptom .

Patient is better in condition or circumstances it denoted as using the symbol ">" or abbreviation "amel"

Importance of modalities – According to Dr. Hahnemann in Aph. No. 18.

Eg. Any 1,2 medicines modalities. (General & particular)

Q. Write about *concordance* or relationship of remedies?

Ans. The word concordance means harmony, synchronization; arrangement in alphabetical order of important words etc.

The word concordance was first of all used by Boenninghausen in homoeopathic literature.

It was replaced by Allen to "Relationship of remedies."

Eg. Gentry concordance repertory.

Q. Write about mental symptoms?

Ans. Definition- Symptoms of mental plane or mind that represent the person as a whole.

1) Will, 2) Understanding, 3) Intellect.

The unique characteristic symptoms of mind will always be considered as peculiar and characteristic symptom of the patient or individual (individualization). This striking symptom helps in finding out the right remedy for easy cure.

Eg. Any 1,2 medicines mental symptoms.

Q. Write about physical general?

Ans. Symptoms of physical plane that represent the person as a whole.

These symptoms can be: Appetite, thirst, desire, aversion, stool, urine, perspiration, addiction, sleep etc.

Eg. Any 1,2 medicines physical general.

Q. Write about particular symptoms?

Ans. Definition- Symptom which are related to a particular part or organ or functions of the body.

Eg. Occiput- Burning pain.

Q. Write about concomitant symptoms?

Ans. Definition- Those symptoms that seemingly have no relation to the leading symptoms or the pathology of the case, yet are present in the patient.

Eg. Any 1,2 medicines concomitant symptoms.

Q. Write about key-note Or Guiding symptoms?

Ans. Definition-Group of symptoms which represent the medicine during prescription.

Keynote characterizes a piece of music.

The same concept has been adopted in homoeopathy. It indicates the identity of the medicine on the basis of which we can individualize and differentiate one medicine from others especially the medicines which are similar in the sphere of action and manifestation.

The term coined by "H.C.Allen."

Q. Write about characteristics or PQRS symptoms?

Ans. UNCOMMON SYMPTOMS.

These are the symptoms on which prescription has to be based upon, It denote those symptoms which are Peculiar, Queer, Rare, Striking in their nature and character.

Which are peculiar to a few patients suffering from similar disease.

Q. Write about drug picture?

Ans. A homoeopathic Materia medica is a collection of "drug pictures", organised alphabetically by "remedy," that describes the symptom patterns associated with individual remedies.

eg. Any 1,2 remedies drug picture.

2 & 5 Marks-

Q.1 Define Homoeopathic Materia Medica?

Q.2 Name the sources of Hom. Materia Medica & Explain?

Q.3 Name the sources of drugs in homoeopathy?

Q.4 Name the 12- Tissue Remedy/ Biochemic Tissue Salts?

Q.5 Name & compare the Trios of remedy-

i) Trios of Restless?

ii) Trios of Pain?

iii) Trios of Burners?

Q.6 Aconite – Common name, Family, Mind, Fear, Causation, Fever.

Q.9 Aethusa – Common name, Family, Mental generals, Epilepsy, Face, Vomiting.

Q.10 Allium cepa – Common name, Family, Eyes, Coryza, Injury.

Q.11 Aloe socotrina – Common name, Family, Skin, Diarrhea, Stool.

Q.12 Antimonium crudum – Common name, Family, Ailments, Desire, Skin, Gen. Modalities.

Q.13 Antimonium tartaricum – Common name, Family, Mental generals, Tongue, Cough?

Q.14 Apis mellifica – Common name, Eyes, Fever, Dropsy, General modalities.

Q.15 Argentum nitricum – Common name, Chemical formula, Constitution, Desire, Craves, Headache, Eyes, Diarrhea.

Q.16 Arnica Montana – Common name, Family, Fever, Skin, Injury, General modalities.

Q.17 Arsenicum album – Common name, Chemical formula, Mental generals, Thirst, Ailments.

Q.18 Arum triphyllum – Common name, Family, Throat, Fever, Cold.

Q.19 Baptisia tinctoria – Common name, Family, Fever, Discharge, Throat, Tongue.

Q.20 Bryonia alba – Common name, family, Ailments, Delirium, Headache, Thirst, Cough, Mastitis.

Q.21 Calcarea carbonica – Common name, Chemical formula, Desire, Longing, Resp. system.

Q.22 Calcarea phosphorica – Common name, Family, Constitution, Ailments.

Q.23 Calendula officinalis – Common name, Family, Injuries.

Q.24 Chamomilla – Common name, Family, Mental generals, Aversion, Face, Convulsion.

Q.25 Cina maritime – Common name, Family, Mental generals, Cravings, Worm complaint, Cough.

Q.26 China officinalis – Common name, Family, Ailments, Headache, Face, Extremity, Fever.

Q.27 Colchicum autumnale – Common name, Family, Ailments, Smell, Aversion, Urine, Rheumatism.

Q.28 Colocynthis – Common name, Family, Mental generals, Colic, Sciatica, Gen. modalities.

Q.29 Drosera rotundifolia – Common name, Family, Cough.

Q.30 Dulcamara – Common name, Family, Mental generals, Ailments, Skin.

Q.31 Euphrasia officinalis – Common name, Family, Eyes.

Q.32 Gelsemium sempervirens – Common name, Family, Mind symptoms, Headache, Heart symptoms, Thirst, Fever.

Q.33 Hepar sulphur – Common name, Chemical formula, Perspiration, Eyes, Throat, Skin, Urinary system.

Q.34 Hypericum perforatum – Common name, Family, Vertigo, Extrimities, Injuries.

Q.35 Ipecacuanha – Common name, Family, Hemorrhage, Cough, Fever, Gen. modalities.

Q.36 Ledum palustre – Common name, Family, Extremities, Face, Injuries.

Q.37 Lycopodium clavatum – Common name, Family, General modalities, G.I.symptoms, Urine, Pneumonia.

Q.38 Magnesium phosphoricum – Common name, Family, Dread, Headache, Ailments, Toothache, Colic, Cramps.

Q.39 Natrium muriaticum – Common name, Family, General modalities, Ailments, Dreams, Craving, Aversion, Headache, Tongue, Fever.

Q.40 Natrium sulphuricum – Common name, Family, General modalities, Skin affection, G.I.complaint , Respiratory complaint.

Q.41 Nux vomica – Common name, Family, Over sensitiveness, Constipation, Convulsion.

Q.42 Pulsatilla nigricans – Common name, Family, General modalities, Constitution, Mental generals, Discharge, Thirst, Eyes.

Q.43 Rhus toxicodendron – Common name, Family, Mental generals, Headache, Tongue, Extremities, Fever.

Q.44 Ruta graveoaalens – Common name, Family, Eyes, G.I.complaint, Skin.

Q.45 Silicea terra – Common name, Family, General modalities, Ailments, Headache, Constipation, Skin.

Q.46 Spongia – Common name, Family, Cough, Heart.

Q.47 Sulphur – Common name, Family, General modalities, Mental generals, Constipation, Menses, Skin.

Q.48 Symphytum officinale – Common name, Family, Injuries.

Q.49 Thuja occidentalis – Common name, Family, General modalities, Constitution, Mental generals, Ailments, Eyes, Constipation, Skin.

10 Marks -

Q.1 Define Homoeopathic Materia Medica and also explain scope and limitation of Homoeopathic Materia Medica.

Q.2 Describe various ways of studying Homoeopathic Materia Medica?

Or Explain different classification of Homoeopathic Materia Medica?

Q.3 Explain principles of Biochemic tissue salts in detail? Name the 12- tissue remedy.

Q.4 How Pulsatilla is useful for female problems in every stage or (sphere) of life.

Q.5 Drug picture / Drug personalities / Characteristic symptoms of –

i.) Aconitum napellus

ii.) Argentum nitricum

iii.) Arsenicum album

iv.) Bryonia alba

v.) Calcarea phosphorica or Cal. Phos. Baby

vi.) Chamomilla or Chamomilla Baby

vii.) Cina maritina or Cina Baby

viii.) Lycopodium clavatum

ix.) Natrium muriaticum

x.) Nux vomica

xi.) Pulsatilla

xii.) Silicea terra or Silicea Baby

xiii.) Sulphur

xiv.) Symphytum officinale

xv.) Thuja occidentalis.

Sources and References

Materia Medica Pura (Dr. C.S.F. Hahnemann)

Allen's Key-notes Rearranged & Classified: With Leading Remedies of the Materia Medica & Bowel Nosodes (H.C. Allen)

All in one Homoeopathic Materia Medica (Prof. Dr. Niranjan Mohanty)